A MAN AFN
HEART

MOVING SUCCESSFULLY TOWARD SPIRITUAL CONTINUITY, ESTABLISHMENT AND LEADERSHIP

McDougal & Associates
Servants of Christ and stewards of the mysteries of God

A MAN AFTER GOD'S OWN
HEART

MOVING SUCCESSFULLY TOWARD SPIRITUAL CONTINUITY, ESTABLISHMENT AND LEADERSHIP

BY

DESMOND ALPHONSO THOMAS

All Scripture quotations are from the Authorized King James Version of the Bible. All scripture word definitions are from *Strong's Exhaustive Concordance* of the Bible, Dugan Publishers, Inc., Gordonsville, Tennessee.

Original cover design by Lara York
zoecreationgrafx@bellsouth.net

Published by:

McDougal & Associates
www.thepublishedword.com

McDougal & Associates is dedicated to the spreading of the Gospel of Jesus Christ to as many people as possible in the shortest time possible.

ISBN 13: 978-0-9543083-1-5
ISBN 10: 0-9543083-1-X

Printed in the United States of America
For Worldwide Distribution

DEDICATION

This book is dedicated to my mentor, the Holy Spirit, who teaches and inspires me everyday through His inner voice and witness and through the Word of God. Thank You, Holy Spirit.

I dedicate this book also to my wife Mary, and my children (Steven, Melchizedek, and Desmond, Jr.) who have sacrificed their husband and father to the propagation of the Gospel to the world.

I also dedicate this book to my Bible College students in Sierra Leone—past, present and future—who trust in my leadership and allow me to be their mentor.

Last, but not least, I also dedicate this book to all who strive for a lasting ministry and for favor with God and man.

ACKNOWLEDGMENTS

I want to thank God for ordering my path by His Holy Spirit every day into the things He has prepared for me.

I want to thank Rev. Harold McDougal whose consistence and undying zeal in ministry has been such a challenge to me. I also want to thank him for his contribution in helping to put this book together. May God bless you and prosper your ministry.

I want to thank people like Myles Monroe and John C. Maxwell whose books and tapes have been such a blessing to me, helping me to realize my leadership abilities.

I want to thank every member of my staff in both Sierra Leone and the United States. God bless you all.

CONTENTS

The LORD hath sought him a man after his own heart, and the LORD hath commanded him to be captain over his people.   1 Samuel 13:14

And thine house and thy kingdom shall be established for ever before thee: thy throne shall be established for ever.   2 Samuel 7:16

INTRODUCTION

What does it really mean to be *a man after [God's] own heart*? What did David have that Saul didn't? Why was Saul rejected and David honored? Why did David find continuity, establishment and a place of leadership among God's people, and Saul did not. There must be an obvious answer to these questions. There must be something that marked one man for failure and the other for greatness.

First, I believe, being a man after God's own heart means being His friend, being close to Him, placing ourselves clearly on His side, following His heart. These days, we're all too easily influenced by the convictions of people around us, especially by those who seem to have a gift of conferring their convictions upon others. We're all persuaded by each other from time to time. But where should our true loyalties lie?

Some are swayed by the sleight of men because they seem not to have any conviction of their own. Jesus called such men *a reed shaken with the wind* (Matthew 11:7). They're like those in the crowd during Jesus' day who were singing hosanna to Him one day and then, just a few days later, were crying out with others, "Crucify

Him!" Whose convictions should we follow: ours, others', or God's?

Some might suggest that we need to follow our own convictions, but our convictions have been influenced by many things, and we can sometimes be convinced by both negative and positive influences. Sometimes we arrive at the wrong conclusion because we don't gather adequate information, and sometimes we err based on our traditions and personal biases. We can never be one hundred percent right on our own because we're only human, and neither omniscient nor omnipresent.

The world around us changes from one theory, or belief, to another. Even science changes. At one time, centuries ago, scientists held the view that the world was flat. Later they realized that they were wrong and that the earth was actually spherical in shape. But we certainly haven't discovered all there is to learn about the earth. Tomorrow some scientific views will again change.

The laws of man are never absolutes. They're modified, changed or discarded with time. Therefore man's conclusions cannot be trusted as absolutes. Even the opinions of those who are sincere and knowledgable are inadequate and can, at times, be sincerely wrong. So who or what can we trust?

One of the main reasons I believe that Christians are criticized today is because of the boldness and authority by which our founder, Jesus Himself, spoke. He always spoke in absolutes. For example, He said very emphatically:

I am the way, the truth, and the life: no man cometh unto the Father, but by me.   John 14:6

Many today criticize the absoluteness of this statement. They would prefer that we said that Jesus is *a* way or *one* way, but not *the* way. But we Christians believe in the absolutes of God, so we cannot change the fact that He is *the* way. We cannot compromise this fact. We believe what the Scriptures say about Him, that He is *"the same yesterday, and to day, and for ever"* (Hebrews 13:8), meaning that the absolutes of His Word cannot change because they are just that—absolutes. He is absolute, or unchanging, and His Word is absolute, or unchanging.

The Bible seems to have always maintained that the world was spherical, even as scientists were professing that it was flat. God should know. He is omnipresent, omniscient, and omnipotent, and that surely guarantees that He will always speak in absolutes. And why shouldn't He?

What I'm trying to express with all of this is that, as believers in Christ, we must base our convictions on God's convictions. This is the reason I encourage every person who loves Him today to become a man or woman after His own heart. His path is proven, and it will lead us to continuity, establishment and exaltation to positions of leadership. To prove that point, we only need note that Christianity continues to be the fastest growing and largest religion in the world and is strongly established in every continent. This is because the Christian Church is built upon the desires of God's heart.

As the main subject of study for this book, we have selected David, for he was the man to whom God referred when He spoke the powerful words of 1 Samuel 13:4. As we shall see, David was truly a man after God's own heart. We will use many other passages of scripture to help us understand this concept better and what it means to you and me today in the twenty-first century.

All around us, Christian men and women are inquiring about the road to success and greatness. They want to know how to be loved and favored by God. These are good questions. God's love is given to each of us without condition, but it is apparent that some people receive more favor from Him than do others. For instance, Jesus loved all His disciples, but John was, perhaps, more beloved than others as he was referred to as *"the disciple whom Jesus loved"* (John 21:20).

There are clearly degrees of grace and mercy. In fact, there are two sides to grace and mercy, and we all have to choose which side we want to be on. We can choose to be on the side of mercy that constantly pleads for forgiveness for sins, or we can choose to receive mercy not to sin in the first place. We can receive grace for salvation only, or we can receive grace for daily living. It is my observation that the secret to greatness with God is to become a seeker of His face. It is when we seek God that all other things are added to us. It is when we know Him that we can do exploits for Him. Jesus said very plainly:

But seek ye first the kingdom of God, and His righteousness; and all these things shall be added unto you.
Matthew 6:33

The prophet Daniel said:

The people that do know their God shall be strong, and do exploits. Daniel 11:32

Learn to seek God as you should, and everything you need will be yours.

The way we get to know God better is through obedience to His Word. Jesus becomes our Lord only when we keep His commandments. He said:

And why call ye me, Lord, Lord, and do not the things which I say? Luke 6:46

If ye love me, keep my commandments. John 14:15

To the other extreme, we stop living when we cease to abide in our God and in His Word, and the result is that we are cast off as a branch that is good for nothing, destined only to be burned (see Matthew 13:40 and Hebrews 6:8). By God's grace, this shall not be our portion. Our portion, rather, is to be pruned, so that we can bear much fruit, fruit that will remain. This is possible only as we seek to be a man or woman after God's own heart.

If that is your desire today, please read on as we examine what caused Saul to fail as king over Israel, why David was chosen to replace him, and what exactly made this man David *A Man After God's Own Heart.*

Desmond A. Thomas
Freetown, Sierra Leone and London, England

13

CHAPTER 1

SAUL'S FALL FROM GRACE

Because thou hast rejected the word of the LORD, he hath also rejected thee from being king.

1 Samuel 15:23

We should see the star of Saul proudly flapping on the flag of Israel today, or some other symbol that denotes his stamp upon the history of that nation and its people. Instead, we see the Star of David. Jesus could well have been called the Son of Saul. Instead, He was called the Son of David. There should have been a long line of kings descending from Saul. Instead, his kingdom came to an abrupt end, and it was David's line that succeeded him, not his own.

For some reason, Saul's reign was not established. There was no continuity to it, and he had no lasting legacy. This is notable because he started out strong, but then something happened that caused him to be removed as king. That something, I am convinced, was the condition of Saul's heart:

And Samuel said [to Saul], When thou wast little in thine own sight, wast thou not made head of the tribes of Israel, and the Lord anointed thee king over Israel?

1 Samuel 15:17

> **God's criterion for exaltation is humility!**

Although Saul was, from his shoulders upward, taller than every other man in Israel, he had not been chosen for his stature. That was a definite bonus, but he was chosen because of the humility of his heart. God's criterion for exaltation is humility. He never honors self-exaltation. He said:

Humble yourselves therefore under the mighty hand of God, that he will exalt you in due time.

1 Peter 5:6

Saul's Mission in Life Defined

Saul's purpose in life was to fight God's battles and establish His Kingdom, and if he was to fail in any area of his life, it must not be in his purpose. He was wired, physically and spiritually, for this unique mission.

At the first, the condition of Saul's heart seemed to be acceptable, and he was blessed to have the guidance of one of the greatest prophets Israel ever knew, the great Samuel. So where did it all go wrong? Did Saul change overnight? Or was there something in his character that had not been dealt with? Can a man be humble and, at

16

the same time, flawed? Personally, I've come to believe that Saul's problem was this: his character flaws caught up with him and destroyed his purpose.

We all have flaws, and if they're not dealt with, they will grow like thorns and choke the very life out of us. Jesus said:

> And the thorns grew up, and choked it [the seed of the Word of God], and it yielded no fruit.   Mark 4:7

Saul's heart was not right with God—even when he was humble. You might ask, "Why, then, did God choose him in the first place?" Well, why did God choose you and me? We have flaws in our character too, and yet He chose us in spite of these flaws. God's will is not that we accept life with our flaws, but rather that we learn to deal with our flaws and overcome them through His grace.

Paul wrote:

> But I keep under my body, and bring it into subjection: lest that by any means, when I have preached to others, I myself should be a castaway.
> 1 Corinthians 9:27

THREE TYPES OF THORNS TO AVOID

The Bibles warns us of three types of thorns, which, if not dealt with, will grow up and choke the Word of God which has been sown into our hearts. They are: *"the cares of this world," "the deceitfulness of riches,"* and *"the lusts of other things"*:

17

And the cares of this world, and the deceitfulness of riches, and the lusts of other things entering in, choke the word and it becometh unfruitful.   Mark 4:19

"Cares," "deceitfulness," and "lusts" ... these are our chief spiritual enemies.

WORRY OR CARE:

If you let worry, or care, have its way, it will come to you every day and eventually overwhelm you. In his writing to the Corinthian believers, Paul wrote of the cares that too often accompany the ministry:

Beside those things that are without, that which cometh upon me daily, the CARE of all the churches.
   2 Corinthians 11:28

Worry in any form is harmful. As a minister, don't even worry about your ministry or your church. Let God take care of them for you. As leaders, we need not worry about anything. Instead, we need to pray and commit our ways to God. The Scriptures teach us:

Be careful for nothing; but in every thing by prayer and supplication with thanksgiving let your requests be made known unto God.   Philippians 4:6

Worrying doesn't change anything. It only adds stress to our lives, and stress can adversely affect our health. Avoid worry at all costs.

18

THE DECEITFULNESS OF RICHES:

Avoid *"the deceitfulness of riches."* Many of us fall into the trap of wanting to get rich quickly and, as a consequence, we allow ourselves to manipulate others and devise all sorts of deceitfulness to reach this desired end. The inevitable end of such actions is the loss of our testimonies and bringing shame to ourselves and to the Gospel of our Lord Jesus Christ.

Please don't be deceived by riches. God doesn't have a problem with you having money, but He does have a problem with money having you. Money is a good servant, but it's a bad master. So don't be deceived by it. All you need to do is to be faithful to God, and He'll reward you. Seek first His Kingdom and His righteousness, and all other things will definitely come to you—in God's time. Money is not a proper motivator for Christian believers.

LUSTS:

Lust is such a destructive force that we must all seek to escape its grasp. Lust could be defined as "an insatiable longing to satisfy negative desires." Lust for anything can damage one's testimony. Don't allow lust to enter in and quench the effectiveness of the Word of God in your life.

Lust for money, position, sex, food and alcohol or many other things can all destroy a ministry, a career, a family, and a testimony. Don't let it happen to you. Stay away from every lust, and if and when you do find yourself enticed, seek deliverance quickly:

> *But every man is tempted, when he is drawn away of his own lust, and enticed.* James 1:14

Escape the corruption that is in the world through lust.   2 Peter 1:4

Saul allowed his flesh to rule his life, and the results were tragic. What's so sad about his story is that he had such a great calling in life.

Knowing Your Calling

As a believer, and especially as a leader, we need to know our calling in life. Why were we placed on this earth? It was to fulfil a particular purpose. Be very careful to identify that call and not to deviate from it or replace it with someone or something else. The moment we allow our purpose to slip from us, we become useless.

If we fail God, He can always find a replacement, but then what happens to us? Losing your purpose makes you fairly worthless in this world. A man fulfilling his purpose is like salt to those around him. He adds taste to this tasteless world and heals the world around him of its wounds:

Salt is good: but if the salt have lost his saltness, wherewith will ye season it? Have salt in yourselves, and have peace one with another.   Mark 9:50

If you can discover your purpose in life, you can change the world around you. If not, you can easily live and die having made little or no impact on the world.

DISCOVERING WHO WE REALLY ARE

We don't know who we really are until we're confronted in a particular area of life. Our reaction in an area of temptation, for instance, reveals what has been stored up in our hearts over time. Saul didn't know how disobedient he could be or how hard it might be for him to carry out explicit instructions until he was faced with the need to do what Samuel had told him to do. His problem had always been there; it was just exposed when he was confronted with the need to obey. Confrontation has a way of bringing out our weaknesses or our strengths.

> *Why were we placed on this earth?*

After I got saved, I began to pray not to be tempted. Then one day the Lord corrected me. If I was never tempted, He told me, there would be no way of knowing my strengths and weaknesses. The secret of our hearts are revealed only when we're confronted with some test of life. Therefore, never despise confrontation, for it reveals your strengths, and it also shows you your weaknesses so that you can work on overcoming them.

Saul's principle mission in life, I believe, was to put an end to the Amalekites. They had been very cruel to God's people and were so scornful of God Himself that He had sworn to eradicate the memory of them from the earth:

21

*And the LORD said unto Moses, Write this for a memo-
rial in a book, and rehearse it in the ears of Joshua: for
I will utterly put out the remembrance of Amalek from
under heaven.*   Exodus 17:14

This explains why God commanded Saul to go out and
kill every last one of the Amalekites. But what did Saul
do?

First, Saul was tested in a battle with the Philistines
(see 1 Samuel 13). In this test, Saul failed miserably. He
stepped outside of his calling and ministry as king and
tried to enter into Samuel's ministry as priest. Then,
when he had made a "mess" of things, he began to make
excuses for his failure.

I'm convinced that each and every one of us is born in
the fullness of time to fulfil God's Word in our generation. Every moment of our lives is a time appointed by
God to establish His written judgements. We are all born
for this express and unique purpose, and so every moment we live is part of God's set time for us. Because of
this, we're the ones who choose whether we will fulfil
God's positive judgements or His negative judgements:

*To execute upon them the judgement written: this hon-
our have all the saints.*   Psalm 149:9

We have no excuse for not executing the positive
judgements written for our case. Saul tried to make excuses, but nothing worked. Now, let's look more closely
at some of his failings:

SAUL MADE EXCUSES

Every time Saul was confronted with wrongdoing, he had some excuse to offer. He was unwilling to confess his sins unless he was forced to do so. Otherwise, he was forever defending his actions.

What does this show us? Was Saul's heart after the people, after himself, or after the Lord? Was he forced into making decisions by pressure from the people around him? As a man chosen by God to lead His people, why was he not more often motivated by God's Spirit?

What would you do if you found yourself in the same situation as Saul? Would you stand alone in your judgement of the truth or would you follow the crowd? Would you find fault, base your decision on assumptions and lies and give in to doing what was not right? That was exactly what Saul did:

> And Samuel said, what hast thou done? And Saul said, Because I saw that the people were scattered from me.
> 1 Samuel 13:11

Saul's first complaint was this: *"The people were scattered from me."* What do you do when you want to stand on the Word of God, but no one else seems to be in the same camp with you? Whose heart do you follow at such a time? Do you dare to stand for what is right? Who controls your decisions, the crowd or God's Word?

Peter was faced with a similar situation in his ministry, and he was also swayed by the crowd. Of him, Paul wrote:

But when Peter was come to Antioch, I withstood him to the face, because he was to be blamed. For before that certain came from James, he did eat with the Gentiles: but when they were come, he withdrew and separated himself, fearing them which were of the circumcision. And the other Jews dissembled likewise with him; insomuch that Barnabas also was carried away with their dissimulation. But when I saw that they walked not uprightly according to the truth of the gospel, I said unto Peter before them all ...

Galatians 2:11-14

> **What makes you a leader is that you're in the lead!**

This was a very sad commentary on a man as great as Peter, and if it happened to him, it can very easily happen to us too. Do you tend to stick with the crowd? This can be tempting, especially when those who seem to be above you in ministry are doing or saying something you see as contrary to the truth of the Gospel.

What makes you a leader is that you're in the lead, not that you're following the lead of others. We need to be men and women after God's own heart and, even in difficult cases, we need to offer some positive guidance.

Time and again, you and I are confronted with having to make a decision in life which may put us on a lonely path and cause us to be unpopular or to lose friends. If we know the truth in such cases, we must stand upon it, and be willing to suffer whatever consequences result.

That's what it means to be a man or woman after God's own heart. Saul chose the easy path.

SAUL FEARED THE PEOPLE

And Saul said to Samuel, I have sinned: for I have transgressed the commandment of the LORD, and thy words: BECAUSE I FEARED THE PEOPLE, AND OBEYED THEIR VOICE.   1 Samuel 15:24

Fear of the crowd is one reason we fail to stand alone in our own good judgement based on the truth of the Gospel. Saul, as leader, was supposed to instruct the people concerning the commandment of the Lord. He was Commander In Chief of his forces, and he was personally responsible for giving instructions to his soldiers and making sure those instructions were carried out. But, because he feared the people, he joined the crowd. And, in doing so, he disobeyed the commandment of the Lord.

Should we ever fail to preach the Word of the Lord because of fear of losing a crow? Should we ever fail to discipline someone influential in the church—even when they're clearly in the wrong? Should we become people-controlled instead of truth-controlled? No! Our focus must always be God and not the people. Are we afraid we will loose popularity with our subordinates? We should always obey God as Ruler, rather than men, and when we do so we can know that He will stand by us, whatever the result.

On one occasion, when I was pastoring our church in the United Kingdom, I observed that a female member of my congregation was going out with a married brother who had recently joined the church. I confronted the two of them and ordered that they discontinue their relationship at once. Instead of heeding my word and being blessed, they became angry with me and left the church.

Years later, I met that sister at a gathering, and she confessed to me and asked my forgiveness for becoming angry and leaving. She admitted that I had been telling her the truth, but she said her pride kept her from accepting my counsel at the time. She had ended the relationship and was now happily married to her own man, and God was blessing the two of them greatly. Stand for the truth, and your adversary will eventually return and bless you. Saul failed to learn this lesson.

Saul Made Decisions Based on Assumption

Therefore said I, The Philistines will come now upon me to Gilgal.   1 Samuel 13:12

It is nowhere recorded that the Philistines did come upon Saul. In fact, in this particular battle, it was Jonathan, Saul's son, who made a daring effort to take the battle to the camp of the Philistines. The Philistines did not attack first. It may be that Saul was just making excuses for his failure or that his fear led him to make a wrong assumption. If we find ourselves in a situation in which we don't know what to do, it's better that we do nothing rather than base our decision on assumption.

As Christians and as Christian leaders, we need to get our facts straight before we make decisions. Decisions based on assumption are usually wrong decisions. Saul should have first gotten his facts right, and because he failed to do this, he felt forced into making an improper decision.

Another area in which many make false assumptions is in our relationships with one another. If someone has not seemed to behave him- or herself well in our presence, we begin to make assumptions about why they have behaved in this way. It would be better to avoid making such assumptions and, instead, to take the bold step of going and asking the person why they have behaved in that manner. Sometimes you'll be surprise at the answers you get. Never assume, but, rather, ask. In this, Saul failed.

SAUL CAST BLAME ON OTHERS

But the people took of the spoil, sheep and oxen, the chief of the things which should have been utterly destroyed.   1 Samuel 15:21

Many people, unwilling to take blame for their own actions, always try to cast blame on others. Saul was often guilty of this. When he stepped out of his ministry and made the sacrifice in Samuel's stead, he chose to blame the people for the wrong done. He also blamed Samuel for not arriving on time. When it was noted that the sheep had not all been slaughtered as commanded, he said that others had been responsible for it. *"The people"* did it, not him.

Saul was a blamer, just as Adam was. Adam blamed

God for giving him a wife who made wrong decisions, and he blamed her for what had gone wrong. Most of us don't have room to accuse others, for we have done the same things.

We men often blame our wives for our failures, and we're quick to blame God for the choice we made for a wife. A man after God's own heart is quick to confess and forsake his own sins, as the Lord Himself admonishes us to do:

> *Confess your faults one to another, and pray one for one another, that ye may be healed.*   James 5:16

(For more important details on this subject of taking responsibility for our own failures, see Chapter 7.)

Some women choose to lay the blame for their failures on their children, and some pastors choose to blame most everything on the members of their congregation. It's always someone else but us—when, in reality, we're the ones who are responsible. Until we stand and take responsibility for our faults and failures, we cannot become the leaders God has intended us to be.

As a leader, we must be able to recognize the fact that we're not invincible. We're subject to faults, just as every other man. The open admission of that fact and the willingness to take full responsibility and suffer the consequences for our actions will make us more of a leader than those who pretend they're invincible when we all know they're not.

Like Peter, even though we may deny the Lord and weep because of it, we must grow to the place that we

SAUL'S FALL FROM GRACE

can confess Him when given another chance. This was
surely what Paul meant when he wrote:

*For behold, ... ye sorrowed after a godly sort. ... What
revenge! In all things ye have approved yourselves to
be clear in this matter.*   2 Corinthians 7:11

Do you need revenge on the
devil? Well, I have good news for
you: it's payback time, and it's
the devil who will have to pay!

Stop pushing the blame for
every failure off onto others,
and start taking a stand for truth
and right. Saul failed this test.

*Some
pastors
choose
to
blame
most
everything
on
the
members
of
their
congregation!*

SAUL LIED TO COVER UP HIS FAILURE

*And Saul said to Samuel, Yea, I
have obeyed the voice of the
LORD, and have gone the way
which the LORD sent me, and
have brought Agag the king of Amalek, and have utterly destroyed the Amalekites.*   1 Samuel 15:20

Why did Saul choose to lie to Samuel? Samuel had
given him specific instructions and he knew what those
instructions were, and yet he compromised. Was he hop-
ing that Samuel would compromise with him?

In other battles, it had been permitted to take spoils,

29

but with this one, it was not permitted. The instructions were very specific: kill everything and everyone. Still, Saul obeyed only in part, and his incomplete obedience cost him the kingdom. He could no longer be captain over God's people because he could not captain his own spirit.

Why was Saul's lie so devastating? This was an important time in the history of Israel. The people needed a leader who could conquer all the lands promised to them and establish the kingdom. And, it seemed, every time they were about to enter into another dimension of the glory of God, they were again faced with Amalek.

Amalek had been the first enemy to fight them when they came out of Egypt, and now, again, they were being confronted by Amalek. In our journey to becoming captain over God's people and also for the continuity and establishment of our calling and ministry, we must all fight Amalek and prevail. Saul failed in this mission.

SAUL LOST HIS PURPOSE IN LIFE

The Amalekites were the descendants of Amalek, a grandson of Esau, and a type of our fleshly lusts. In our journey to our destiny in life, we must first of all fight the Amalek within before we can face the Amalek without. If we fail to fight and destroy our own fleshy desires, they can easily defeat us and destroy our purpose in life. If, before we can get started dealing with life's more serious issues, we make the decision to fight and conquer ourselves, then (and only then) are we ready for our journey to success.

Many times our defeats do not come from our external enemies. They come as a result of our own weaknesses and failures. We must destroy our own lust in our climb to love, which is the desired pinnacle of our perfection as children of God. As Peter wrote to the Church:

Whereby are given unto us exceeding great and precious promises: that by these ye might be partakers of the divine nature, having escaped the corruption that is in the world through lust. 2 Peter 1:4

Saul failed to destroy his Amalek, and the result was that he also failed to fulfil his purpose on the earth. From the moment of his disobedience, everything began to go downhill for him.

Whatever you do, don't fail to fulfil your singular and unique purpose and object in life. Losing your purpose is like salt that has lost its savor. It is, Jesus said, *"good for nothing"*:

It is thenceforth good for nothing, but to be cast out, and to be trodden under foot of men. Matthew 5:13

Saul now had no purpose, so God had to take the kingdom from him and give it to his neighbor. If we replace our purpose with our lust, we will also be replaced.

One of the reasons Jehu, in the later history of Israel, was anointed king over the people was so that he could pass the judgement decreed by God upon the house of Ahab for the sins that wicked king had committed.

Although Jehu was an unrighteous man, because he carried out his objective in slaying Ahab's house, God granted four generations of his descendants to reign after him as kings over Israel:

Whatever you do, don't fail in your objective in life!

And the LORD said unto Jehu, Because thou hast done well in executing that which is right in mine eyes, and hast done unto the house of Ahab according to all that was done in mine heart, thy children unto the fourth generation shall sit on the throne of Israel.

2 Kings 10:30

Whatever you do, don't fail in your objective in life. Your very existence depends on it. Saul was never able to grasp this truth.

SAUL WANTED TO DO GOD'S WORK ON HIS OWN TERMS

God will accept any work done in His name and based on His Word, but He will not accept any work on our terms, especially when it contradicts something He has said in His Word. And that was Saul's problem. He wanted to do the work of the Lord, but on his own terms.

As we saw, his first excuse was that the Philistines were coming after him, and he had not made supplication unto the Lord (see 1 Samuel 13:12). His next excuse was that they had spared the best of the sheep to offer sacrifices to the Lord. Samuel did not just call these actions foolishness; he called them *"rebellion," "stubbornness,"* and *"witchcraft":*

> *And Samuel said, Hath the LORD as great delight in burnt offerings and sacrifices, as in obeying the voice of the LORD? Behold, to obey is better than sacrifice, and to hearken than the fat of rams. For rebellion is as the sin of witchcraft, and stubbornness is as iniquity and idolatry. Because thou hast rejected the word of the LORD, he hath also rejected thee from being king.*
> 1 Samuel 15:22-23

Any work a person professes to do in the name of the Lord on his own terms is nothing short of witchcraft. There are many examples of this. For instance, these days, many go to war, killing and committing other atrocities, all in the name of the Lord. But we never do Him a favor by breaking His commandments, and we must never do something evil in His name. If God is the God He professes to be, then He can fight His own battles. In fact, He has told us clearly that vengeance belongs to Him; He will repay:

> *Dearly beloved, avenge not yourselves, but rather give place unto wrath: for it is written, Vengeance is mine; I will repay, saith the Lord.*   Romans 12:19

It is utterly amazing how very many Christians take

things into their own hands these days, doing things that are clearly not right—and doing them in the name of the Lord. One lady told of going to a certain pastor for prayer because she could not become pregnant. The minister told her that *he* would be the one who could make her pregnant, not her husband. What a false prophet he turned out to be!

Adultery never gives birth to deliverance. This was just another form of the witchcraft we're talking about here. You can never bring about the purpose of God through sin. You cannot do evil and expect good to come from it. Paul declared that God will punish all who do such things, regardless of their titles:

> *But we are sure that the judgment of God is according to truth against them which commit such things. And thinkest thou this, O man, that judgest them which do such things, and doest the same, that thou shalt escape the judgment of God?* Romans 2:2-3

Saul failed to understand these truths.

Saul Failed to Realize that Obedience Is Always *"Better"*

If we want to work for God, we have to do things His way. We have to obey His voice. Obedience is *"better"* than any sacrifice we could possibly offer Him. In fact, we would never have to make any sacrifice to God for sins at all, if we obeyed Him in the first place.

If Adam had obeyed God in the Garden of Eden, there

34

would have been no need for Jesus to come into the world and sacrifice His life for the sins of mankind. Obedience in Eden would have eliminated the need for Calvary.

Many Christians see Calvary as our ultimate goal, but our goal as Christians is not Calvary, but God's glory. Calvary only restores us to our place of beginnings, and from there we must continue to our full purpose in life. That purpose is glorification in Christ.

If we obey God's Word, we gain His trust, and if we're faithful to one another, we gain each other's trust. But when we miss the mark, we then have to try again and again to regain lost trust. All the time we spend in regaining trust would not be necessary if we were obedient in the first place.

You have a choice, so choose obedience. God delights in obedience more than in sacrifice. Therefore, never make the mistake of trying to replace obedience with sacrifice.

If someone has to always make up for a fault with a gift, he doesn't truly love. He's only offering a bribe. Never confuse love with bribes. God delights in your obedience more than in your gifts.

Although giving is important to God, don't make the mistake of tarnishing your giving with sin. Your sinning can easily cancel every benefit of your giving.

Samuel said, *"To hearken is better than the fat of rams."* Our service to God must be on the basis of obedience to His commands. We need to be men and women who seek after His heart and obey His voice. Don't be guilty of abusing His grace.

As I noted in the Introduction, grace and mercy both have two sides. You can believe God for His grace not to sin, or you can seek His grace once you have sinned. In the same way, you can believe God for His mercy to *present your bodies a living sacrifice, holy, acceptable unto God"* (Romans 12:1), or you can be in the place of asking for His mercy for your continuing sin. I am reminded of the powerful words of the apostle Paul:

> *What shall we say then? Shall we continue in sin, that grace may abound? God forbid. How shall we, that are dead to sin, live any longer therein? Know ye not, that so many of us as were baptized into Jesus Christ were baptized into his death? Therefore we are buried with him by baptism into death: that like as Christ was raised up from the dead by the glory of the Father, even so we also should walk in newness of life. For if we have been planted together in the likeness of his death, we shall be also in the likeness of his resurrection: knowing this, that our old man is crucified with him, that the body of sin might be destroyed, that henceforth we should not serve sin. For he that is dead is freed from sin.* Romans 6:1-7

God is calling every man, woman, boy and girl alive today to be obedient to Him, so let obedience be your first choice. Chastisement, which is uncomfortable for any of us, comes to us only when we have failed to obey Him in the first place. Chose obedience, and you can avoid chastisement.

Administering discipline to us is a painful experience

even for God, and He won't have to go that far if we obey. To recover from the shame and disgrace of His displeasure is often a painful experience, one that many are unwilling to face, and so they simply quit the Kingdom. Obedience is always *"better,"* so choose to obey. Saul did not.

SAUL *"FORCED"* HIMSELF IN THE WRONG DIRECTION

I forced myself therefore and offered the burnt offering.
1 Samuel 13:12

God would much rather you forced yourself to obey Him than that you forced yourself to obey your own voice or the voice of the people around you. Resist being pressured into doing things that you know are not God's will— whether the pressure comes from parents, peers, or the majority opinion of the day. If you give in to others, you'll always regret it. Whatever you do, don't let others determine your destination in life. Let God alone do that.

You can believe God for His grace not to sin, or you can seek His grace once you have sinned!

In all these ways, Saul showed that he was not really a man after God's own heart. He was more of a people pleaser, a man who allowed his own desires and those of others around him to overrule God's best for his life. This, of course, led to the tragedy and loss. May this not be the ending of your story. ♥

CHAPTER 2

WHY DID GOD CHOOSE DAVID TO REPLACE SAUL?

[Samuel] looked on Eliab, and said, Surely the Lord's anointed is before him. But the Lord said unto Samuel, Look not on his countenance, or on the height of his stature; because I have refused him: for the LORD *seeth not as man seeth; for man looketh on the outward appearance, but the* LORD *looketh on the heart.*

1 Samuel 16:6-7

When Saul was chosen to be Israel's first king, it was duly noted that he was a big man, very impressive, head and shoulders above the rest, but David was just the opposite. He was not only young; he was shorter than Saul. His own brothers and his very father discounted him as a viable candidate. Even the prophet Samuel saw David's elder brother Eliab as a more suitable leader for the nation. Why, then, did God reject Eliab and choose David to replace the disgraced King Saul?

On what basis do we choose our successors, partners, husbands, wives, and associates? Many times we look on the intellectual and physical attributes of the person,

39

rather than looking on their heart. We need to be spiritual to be able to see the heart, although sometimes we can determine its worth by the fruit it inspires.

God sees and knows the secrets of every human heart:

> *Shall not God search this out? for he knoweth the secrets of the heart.*   Psalm 44:21

We need God to reveal to us what He already knows about a person so that we can make better choices in life.

God needed someone to succeed Saul, and He sent Samuel to choose someone. This was a difficult decision for Samuel because he felt that he had made one wrong choice, and he didn't want to make another one. Still, he nearly failed again. Like us, Samuel was tempted to base his choice on the obvious qualifications of a candidate, the appearance of physical and intellectual mastery.

Thankfully, he was a prophet, and when the Lord spoke to him and corrected him, this enabled him to make the right choice for Israel.

LOOKING AS AN INTELLECTUAL EXERCISE

According to *Strong's,* the Hebrew word *Raah,* translated here in 1 Samuel 16:7 as *"look on,"* carries the meaning "to view, perceive, or see intellectually." How very often we perceive things only from an intellectual perspective and not from a spiritual one. When doing God's business, we must sense the will of His Spirit. And

His will frequently does not agree with our own first impressions.

Eliab seemed to have the intellectual and physical attributes of a king, but he did not possess the heart of one. Therefore, he was rejected from being king over Israel. God always chooses on the basis of the heart, never the intellect.

Concerning the husband or wife you have married or want to marry, have you examined their heart? Or are you simply attracted by their physical appearance or their intellectual ability? Concerning the assistant pastor you've chosen or are considering choosing, what is or what will be the basis for your choice? Will it be because of intellect or charisma, or will you, like Samuel, choose a person who pleases God?

Saul was blessed with physical stature, but as we noted in the previous chapter, he was not chosen on that basis. Physical and intellectual strengths are a bonus, but they can never be the basis for selection.

> *God always chooses on the basis of the heart, never the intellect!*

So how was David chosen? He was chosen because his heart was open to God. He sought after God's will more than anything else in life. He was a man after God's own heart.

In his times private devotion, when no one was watching or listening, David sang to God:

As the hart panteth after the water brooks, so panteth my soul after thee, O God.

My soul thirsteth for God, for the living God: when shall I come to appear before God.   Psalm 42:1-2

This thirst for God was the thing that led to David's being chosen. It happened in this way.

God showed Samuel which house to go to, that of a man named Jesse, but the problem was that Jesse had many sons. When none of the older sons suited God, Jesse's youngest son, a lad named David, was then called for:

And he sent and brought him in. Now he was ruddy, and withal of a beautiful countenance, and goodly to look to. And the LORD said, Arise, anoint him: for this is he.   1 Samuel 16:12-13

And that was final! God was pleased with David, and so David, not Eliab or some other tall, handsome man, was chosen as Israel's next king. Clearly, God sees things differently than we do.

LOOKING FROM A SPIRITUAL PERSPECTIVE

In 1 Samuel 16:7, there is a second use of the phrase "look on." This time, it is not the Hebrew word *Raah*; it is *Ayin*. According to *Strong's,* this word means: "to afflict, in the sense of something acted upon by an outside force, as an eye is by light." It also means: "an outer reflection of an inward attitude." When we allow the eye of our heart to come into contact with the light of God's Word and it does not repel that light, then we begin to become men and women after God's own heart.

When we do this, we begin to put on an outward reflection of God's grace and favor which is capable of preparing us for promotion as one of God's captains and giving us continuity and establishment in our life's endeavors. David prepared himself in the fields, allowing God to penetrate his heart with His Word without resistance. And that is what God saw as the basis for his promotion:

David was good looking in his own right, as had been Saul. They both had beautiful exteriors, but God was clearly more concerned with the condition of the heart.

Being physically ugly does not qualify one to be used by God, but neither does it mean automatic rejection. In the same way, physical beauty does not automatically guarantee a person a place in God's service, but it also does not mean that they must be automatically rejected. In both cases, we must *look on* the heart.

There is an intellectual way to look at things, and that is what man most often choose, but there is also a looking that is done from the spiritual perspective, God's perspective, and that should be our choice.

"GOODLY TO LOOK TO"

David was "goodly to look to." According to *Strong's*, this phrase, translated from the Hebrew word *Tov*, means: "pleasant," "beautiful," "excellent," "fruitful," "righteous," and "moral goodness." This is what God saw when he looked at David, and David wasn't always in Church. God saw him as righteous in his daily living.

How much does God's Word affect you in your daily living? Do you choose to obey God in the details of everyday life? Does God's Word affect your behavior on your job, in the way you relate to your spouse, in the way you choose to raise your children?

> *Do you choose to obey God in the details of everyday life?*

There is nothing like the power of the Word of God to establish your ways. Do you want to be God's captain? Then you need continuity and establishment, and nothing stands forever like the Word of the Lord. All other rules, precepts, and ideologies of men are like grass and flowers that eventually fade away. It is only the Word of God that never changes. So choose God's Word, and in doing so, choose to be a man or woman after His own heart.

Such a decision will make you stand out from the crowd. David was in the fields feeding and otherwise caring for his father's sheep and was not even under consideration by his parents in the selection process for king. But a man after God's own heart cannot remain hidden for very long. The Lord, who sees *"in secret,"* will always reward you *"openly"* (Matthew 6:18).

If you stand the test of God's Word when no one is watching you, then you've already become a candidate for exaltation before men. You may not be counted in man's selection process for promotion, but God will overrule the plans of men and exalt you anyway. So if you're faithful to God's Word in little things, you've already positioned yourself for greatness and promotion. And the more God and His Word penetrates your heart, the more His presence will be with you to propel you toward greatness.

If you seek God's face, His hand will always be there to help you. He has promised you *"all ... things"* (Matthew 6:33).

DAVID HAD LONG BEEN ANOINTED KING

In David's case, he was anointed king long before he actually took the throne. During the intervening years, as David sought God, God continued to make a way for him to obtain that for which he was anointed. People around him began to see what he was "wired" for, and they began to put him into contact with the people who could take him where he was going.

Here's an example of what God did for David:

And Saul said unto his servants, Provide me a man that can play well, and bring him to me. Then answered one of the servants, and said, Behold I have seen a son of Jesse the Bethlehemite, that is cunning in playing, and a mighty valiant man, and a man of war, and prudent in matters, and a comely person, and the LORD is with him. 1 Samuel 16:17-18

When you seek God's face continually and allow His Word to penetrate your heart, He will place His anointing upon you. This will cause people around you to see your gift, and they will make mention of you to others who can propel you to your place in life. You never need to buy, or bribe, you way, betray someone else, or sell yourself to get to the top. God will do it all for you.

Again, how did you choose your spouse? Was your choice based on intellectual maturity? Was it based on physical attractiveness? Was it because he or she was "sexy"? Was it based on how broad his chest was or how full her bust was? All of that seems good and important to us humans, but the most important thing we might look for is what place the Word of God has in the life of the person we're considering as a possible life mate. If that person's heart attracts the Word of God, then he or she is a candidate worth considering. They have what the Bible calls, *"The fear of the Lord"*:

> *The fear of the LORD is the beginning of wisdom: a good understanding have all they that do his commandments: his praise endureth for ever.*   Psalm 111:10

THE HEART IS THE CENTER OF A MAN'S EXISTENCE

Man is a spirit being. His heart is the very center of his existence, what makes him who he is. At salvation, it is the heart of man that is saved. We became *"a new creature"* in Christ by having a change of heart:

> *Therefore if any man be in Christ, he is a new crea-*

46

ture: *old things are passed away; behold, all things are become new.* 2 Corinthians 5:17

If our heart is right with God, we're already positioned for Him to use us. A regenerated heart, or a heart with new life, only needs to present its corporal body as a living sacrifice to God and have its mind renewed by the Word of God, as Paul taught the Roman believers:

I beseech you therefore, brethren, by the mercies of God, that ye present your bodies a living sacrifice, holy, acceptable unto God, which is your reasonable service. And be not conformed to this world: but be ye transformed by the renewing of your mind, that ye may prove what is that good, and acceptable, and perfect, will of God. Romans 12:1-2

Jeremiah described an unregenerate heart:

The heart is deceitful above all things, and desperately wicked: who can know it? Jeremiah 17:9

Solomon warned such a person:

Rejoice, O young man, in thy youth; and let thy heart cheer thee in the days of thy youth, and walk in the ways of thine heart, and in the sight of thine eyes: but know thou, that for all these things God will bring thee into judgement. Ecclesiastes 11:9

The heart is where the seeds of all sorts of works are

sown, and it is in the heart that these seeds take root and grow. Then, what grows in the heart determines the fruit the flesh produces:

THE CONDITION OF THE HEART
DETERMINES FRUITFULNESS

Jesus showed us the truth of this, when He said:

Do not ye yet understand, that whatsoever entereth in at the mouth goeth into the belly, and is cast out into the draught? But those things which proceed out of the mouth come forth from the heart; and they defile the man. For out of the heart proceed evil thoughts, murders, adulteries, fornications, thefts, false witness, blasphemies: these are the things which defile a man. Matthew 15:17-20

As He showed us in His sermon on the mount, the heart will inevitably follow what it treasures:

For where your treasure is, there will your heart be also. Matthew 6:21

An unregenerate heart will treasure wicked and deceitful things. It will love sin and live in it comfortably, but a regenerate heart can no longer delight in sin. It has been born of God:

Whosoever is born of God doth not commit sin; for his seed remaineth in him: and he cannot sin, because he is born of God. 1 John 3:9

The regenerate heart will not only refrain from sin; it will, in fact, warn you of sin. Sometimes believers choose not to listen to their heart, and they go on sinning anyway, but any true child of God cannot last long in sin. They will soon find their way back to righteousness.

THE MOUTH SPEAKS WHAT THE HEART STORES

The mouth speaks what the heart stores. Jesus said:

> *The mouth speaks what the heart stores!*

O generation of vipers, how can ye, being evil, speak good things? for out of the abundance of the heart the mouth speaketh. A good man out of the good treasure of the heart bringeth forth good things: and an evil man out of the evil treasure bringeth forth evil things.

Matthew 12:34-35

Saul lied because lies were stored up in his heart. But lies can never find a place in the godly heart, therefore they do not stay around for long. Saul's continuous denial of the truth and his continuous devising of lies proves what kind of heart he had.

THE HEART DETERMINES THE QUALITY OF OUR WORSHIP

True worship comes only from a pure heart:

But the hour cometh, and now is, when the true wor-
shippers shall worship the Father in spirit and in truth:
for the Father seeketh such to worship him. God is a
Spirit: and they that worship him much worship him
in spirit and in truth.   John 4:23-24

You cannot continue in true worship of God and have sin in your heart. He is a holy God whose presence cannot be approached by those who are contaminated with sin. A regenerate heart will convict you of any sin that may be present in you as you attempt to approach the presence of God. In these cases, it is your own heart that is convicting you.

Our heart is at work in many spiritual activities. We worship God *"in spirit,"* or with our heart. We receive faith, believe, or receive revelation knowledge with our heart. And the place where we are convinced of wrongdoing is in our heart. If our worship is right, we can hear from God. If our convictions are right, then we can say that our heart is right with God. This being true, we will have positioned ourselves for God to use us and to entrust to us an established and continuing ministry.

THE HEART IS CHALLENGED
BY THE POWER OF MEDIATION

I regularly test and tune my heart with the power of meditation. My body wars against my heart. It rebels against its holy desire. It does not want me to meditate on the promises of the sacred Scriptures.

My flesh wants sin to dominate my spirit, and the

man of flesh wants to take control of the spirit man. But I notice that the more I meditate and believe in the God's words and receive them into my heart, the more I break the desire for sin in my flesh. Determine to meditate on the word of your righteousness until it is manifested in your flesh.

Keeping the Heart Requires Diligence

Keep thy heart with all diligence; for out of it are the issues of life.   Proverbs 4:23

Wherefore the rather, brethren, give diligence to make your calling and election sure: for if you do these things you shall never fall.   2 Peter 1:10

There is a battle going on for our heart. This battle is being waged by our flesh and our mind, and we must win this battle at any cost. You simply must defend your heart against sin. You cannot remain passive in this fight. If you are not diligent in this respect, you will surely fall.

Be on the lookout for the enemy's approach, and do not encourage him in any way. Don't give him any form of control over you. Guard the entrance to your heart so that he is unable to gain a foothold.

Nothing is more important than these issues of the heart. Therefore each of us must be diligent to pray, to fast, and to meditate on God's Word. This is the way we can guard ourselves against sin. If you are found faithful in these simple things, you will be well on your way to an established ministry.

Are you being diligent enough in this regard? Cut off anything that offends you. You can do without it. Make a straight path for your feet. He who does these things shall never fall. As Peter wrote to the Church:

> *And besides this, giving all diligence, add to your faith virtue; and to virtue knowledge; and to knowledge temperance; and to temperance patience; and to patience godliness; and to godliness brotherly kindness; and to brotherly kindness charity.* 2 Peter 1:5-6

When God looked at David, He saw his heart, and He knew that David was His man!

Be sure to add to your faith today.

It was apparently difficult for many people in David's day to see why he, of all people, should be chosen to replace the disgraced King Saul. But God knew. When the people looked at David, they saw his youth and inexperience, his smallness, his apparent strangeness. After all, there must be something wrong with a person who sits on a hillside strumming a little harp and singing to sheep. But when God looked at David, he saw his heart. He saw righteousness and goodness, and He knew that David was His man.

David was indeed a man after God's own heart, and that was qualification enough for what God was calling him to. The rest would come.

Let us continue to look at the strengths that made David *A Man After God's Own Heart.* ♥

CHAPTER 3

UNDERSTANDING YOUR COVENANT WITH GOD

A MAN AFTER GOD'S OWN HEART UNDERSTANDS HIS COVENANT WITH THE ALMIGHTY.

And David spoke to the men that stood by him, saying, ... Who is this uncircumcised Philistine, that he should defy the armies of the living God?
1 Samuel 17:26

Many of the elements necessary to success in the Christian life and ministry are demonstrated in the age-old story of David and Goliath. First, it shows the need for the right opportunity.

THE RIGHT OPPORTUNITY

Having God's favor upon your life is not all you need to bring you to a place of prominence. You'll also need opportunity, and you'll need preparation so that when the right opportunity presents itself, you'll be ready.

When favor meets opportunity and preparedness, there's no stopping you.

David had his moments of preparation in the field when confronted by a bear and a lion that threatened his flock. He trusted God to help him and he rose up and was able to kill them both. He had become a man of war long before he fought Goliath. Saul just didn't know it yet. All David needed was the opportunity to serve in Saul's army so that he could show his strength. He had been preparing for this day for years.

> *David had become a man of war long before he fought Goliath!*

If David's skills in war had not taken him to Saul's palace, his musical talent would surely have taken him there anyway. The Scriptures declare:

> *A man's gift maketh room for him, and bringeth him before great men.*   Proverbs 18:16

If you're a person after God's heart, just be strong in your gift and wait for your God-given opportunity. It will be coming your way soon enough.

The key to greatness and favor with God, as we noted early on, is to be a seeker of His face and not just a seeker of His hand. Be a seeker of His ways, not simply of His acts. In short, seek first His Kingdom, and then all the things you need will be *"added unto you."*

Never seek things. They will lead you away from the search for God's face. It is as you seek God and stand in obedience to His Word that He will present you with an opportunity for success in life.

People who have been preparing for their opportunity will notice it, even though it is hidden in some far corner. Those who have failed to prepare for their opportunity will not be able to identify it when it comes, even if it happens to be standing at their front door. Opportunity comes often to for those who are looking for it.

Opportunity Is Accompanied by Opposition

We must all understand, however, that opportunity often comes accompanied by opposition. Those who have an eye for opportunity will either despise or challenge the opposition that accompanies it. We must set our eyes, not on the opposition, but on the opportunity. There is a price to pay for every victory.

Those who make good use of opportunities are said by some to be "lucky." But someone has described "luck" as being the moment when preparedness meets opportunity. Make sure you're ready, and your opportunity will come.

Focus on the prize:

Looking unto Jesus the author and finisher of our faith; who for the joy that was set before him endured the

cross, despising the shame, and is set down at the right
hand of the throne of God. Hebrews 12:2

Jesus was not looking at the shame of the cross, regardless of how shameful it was; He was looking at the
prize of the cross. He despised the shame of the cross to
gain the joy that was set before Him in leading many
sons into glory. Now, He is at an exalted place of glory
and authority with the Father in Heaven. Your moment
of opportunity will come too.

The Day of Opportunity Arrives

David's opportunity finally came:

And David spoke to the men that stood by him, say-
ing, What shall be done to the man that killeth this
Philistine, and taketh away the reproach from Israel? ...
And the people answered him after this manner, say-
ing, So shall be done to the man that killeth him.
1 Samuel 17:26-27

"What shall be done to the man that killeth this Philis-
tine?" David was looking for an opportunity, and that's
why he asked this question. What would he benefit from
killing the giant? He was not interested in killing; he was
asking for an opportunity to glorify God and to show
forth his gifts.

And the opportunity was there. Goliath was his opportunity. In any adversity, there is an opportunity, and if we
face life with this attitude, we will surely win every time.

David only needed a little motivation, something to stir him to do battle with this giant of a man, something he could focus on as a prize. This would encourage him to fight well and to win.

And the motivation was there: the man who fought Goliath and won would marry the king's daughter, and his father's house would be freed from paying any further taxes. In this, David saw an opportunity to become a prince, live in Saul's palace, and to be free from financial burden. He did not hesitate for a moment, but grabbed his opportunity. And each of us must do the same.

God gives opportunities to every living soul, but it's up to us to lay hold of them. Your opportunity may be quite different from David's, but it's coming. Look for it. You will have an opportunity to become a blessing to someone in your everyday life. Don't wait for a larger platform. Take that opportunity.

When someone around us is sick, we who have God's power should see it as an opportunity to pray for them and see them restored to health. Our reward at the moment may only be to see joy return to their countenance. But in doing that, we have moved up God's ladder to success and greater opportunity. Don't despise any opportunity.

Anytime a missionary offering is being raised in our churches, we should look upon it as an opportunity to help lost souls come to Christ. Our giving must not be done only with the idea of receiving a return on our heavenly investment, although the receiving part of our giving should be evident to all. If our giving can bring others joy, then we should forget our momentary suffering and let that joy be the motivation for our sacrifice. By obeying God in the offering, you are preparing yourself for greater service.

Success is not determined by how much strength or wisdom we possess, nor by how skillful we might become. We can possess strength, skill, learning, and favor, but if God does not give us an opportunity, all of these will not matter. The wise Solomon declared:

> *I return and saw under the sun, that the race is not for the swift, nor the battle to the strong, neither yet bread to the wise, nor yet riches to men of understanding, nor yet favour to men of skill; but time and chance happeneth to them all.* Ecclesiastes 9:11

There are many people living today who hold doctorate degrees, and yet they struggle to pay their monthly bills. There are many ladies living today who are beautiful, and yet they can't seem to find a proper mate. There are many swift runners on the continents of Africa and Asia, and yet most of them will never have a chance to be entered in the Olympics or some great marathon. Why? It all boils down to opportunity or the lack of it. It makes all the difference in the world.

Your opportunity is coming.

THE RIGHT TIMING

> *But time and chance happeneth to them all.*
> Ecclesiastes 9:11

There is time for every purpose and for every work.
Ecclesiastes 3:17

Timing is another element necessary for success. God makes everything beautiful in its time. When it's not yet our time, things may not seem very beautiful. During the time a butterfly waits as a cater- pillar, its life doesn't seem very beautiful. Then it springs forth.

You have a purpose, and there is a time for that purpose. There- fore you must wait on the Lord for that perfect timing.

Take, for example, the mango tree. It doesn't matter what you do to it, the tree simply will not pro- duce before its time. You can put additional manure around it and water it more than usual, but still it will only produce fruit in its season.

> *When it's not yet our time, things may not seem very beautiful!*

We all have a particular season, and if yours hasn't yet come, it's only a matter of time. So just keep doing the right thing, and the Lord will give you your opportunity and your season.

It's possible, as happened with David, to have a recog- nized call to the ministry and even be anointed for it, and yet the time to reign has not yet come. When this is the case, it means that we need to be under the ministry of someone else for a time, for the purpose of teaching and tu- torship. This will continue until the time appointed by our Father.

Don't fail to wait for that appointed time. Refuse to give birth to your baby before its due. Wait on your ministry.

THE RIGHT ATTITUDE

David was shorter than Saul, but his attitude placed him head and shoulders above others. If we're to live in this earth as victors and not victims, if we're live as overcomers and not those who are overcome, and if we're to reign in life as kings and not be subjected to all of life's ills, we need to develop the attitude of champions. If you think that the whole world is against you, that you were born on the wrong side of the globe to succeed, that your skin is the wrong color, and that you have the wrong postal code for success, your attitude will defeat your purpose. You cannot be more than your attitude allows:

> *As [a man] thinketh in his heart, so is he.*
> Proverbs 23:7

A failure attitude will make you a failure, and a winning attitude will make you a winner. You were created to be a winner and to be blessed. God had endowed you with the ability to be fruitful, to multiply, and to subdue the earth, so let these truths form in you a corresponding attitude.

David was ready. He had the right opportunity, the right timing and the right attitude. That uncircumcised Philistine had to go.

FACING DOWN THE UNCIRCUMCISED

Who is this uncircumcised Philistine?   1 Samuel 17:26

The uncircumcised should never be allowed to bring reproach upon the circumcised. If the reproach of sin—sickness, poverty, defeat, failure, disappointment etc.—remains in the life of a believer, something is wrong. Either they don't understand their covenant with God, or they have failed to recognize the opportunities God has placed along their way. It's time, and your opportunity is at the door. If a giant accompanies your opportunity, step forth and slay him.

David saw Goliath as his opportunity and knew that he had to fall. Others looked upon him and decided that he was just too big to kill, but David saw him as just too big to miss with one of the stones from his faithful sling. That was typical of his winning attitude.

This word *uncircumcised,* as David used it here, means "not in covenant with God." David knew that he was in covenant with God through the circumcision of his flesh. By that act carried out in faith, he had a covenant relationship with the Almighty.

David knew that he possessed the blessing of Abraham to prosper in whatever he put his hand to:

Whatsoever he doeth shall prosper.   Psalm 1:3

He knew that he, fighting alone, could put a thousand to flight:

How should one chase a thousand, and two put ten thousand to flight, except their Rock had sold them, and the LORD had shut them up?

> Deuteronomy 32:30

He understood that the Angel of God was camping around him and his people to protect them:

The angel of the LORD encampeth round about them that fear him, and delivereth them. Psalm 34:7

> *It was this covenant consciousness that caused David to roll away the reproach from Israel that day!*

It was this covenant consciousness that caused David to roll away the reproach from Israel that day.

And what about you? Do you have a covenant with God. Do you know what is yours? If not, why not? Do you understand your covenant with God against the sin that so easily besets you? Do you know His promise that sin shall not have dominion over you because you are under grace? Do you know what your covenant is with God concerning that "uncircumcised" sickness that tries to come upon you? Do you know that by His stripes you are healed?

Do you understand that through your covenant with God you have authority over the demons that torment you? If you know your covenant with God, you will rise up from the thing that wants to bring reproach and defeat to you. In the name of Jesus, your Savior, do as David did with the Philistine giant. Command that thing to die. And it will die—in Jesus' name.

God is a God of covenant. He's the initiator of the very concept of covenant. He loves covenant, and if you will search His heart, you will see covenant written there. Know your covenant with God, apply its tenants to your daily living, and you will be known as a friend of God.

Abraham, David, and Solomon all understood their covenant with God, and they became His friends. Dare to be His friend today.

As he approached the area of battle that days, David knew his covenant with God, and he stepped into it. Today, this man is remembered for many things, but the thing that most of us remember him for (even little children) is that he slew Goliath. In the future, you will also be known for the covenant promises you apply to your everyday life.

Don't waste time listening to God's Word if you're unwilling to apply it. It will only do you good when it has been applied. Don't just eat the meat of God's Word; digest it, and when it's made flesh, it will add life and health to you to your bones.

THE WORLD SEES COVENANT AS ARROGANCE

And Eliab his eldest brother heard when he spake unto the men; and Eliab's anger was kindled against David, and he said, Why cameth thou down hither? And with whom hast thou left those few sheep in the wilderness? I know thy pride, and the naughtiness of thine heart;

*for thou art come down that thou mightest see the battle.
And David said, What have I now done? Is there not a
cause?*   1 Samuel 17:28-29

God rejected Eliab from being king, for He saw the man's heart, and it did not match His requirements. Now, we see Eliab severely criticizing David. He accused David of *"pride"* and *"naughtiness of heart."* And David was just trying to do the right thing.

This word *"pride"* used here could also be translated as "naughtiness, arrogance, insolence, and rebelliousness." The pride of which Eliab spoke is one that presumes to have more authority than is warranted, one in which disobedience is inevitable. *Naughtiness* denotes "a heart with an evil condition or negative attitude."

Isn't it amazing that the heart God commended others condemned. The heart God said was right with Him others said was wrong. Have you observed the fact that when you stand in your covenant with God, you will not only experience opposition from the adversary? No! You will also have opposition from your brethren in the Church. For some unknown reason, they now oppose you—criticizing, judging, and condemning your motives, faith, and confession.

When you decide to get out of the comfort zone of the Christians around you and step out in faith, you are judged as one presuming to have more authority than is warranted. If you listen to such complaints, you will stay in the same reproach with the scorners. David reminded his elder brother of God's promise to Israel: *"Is there not a cause?"*

What is your motivation in life? Who are you waiting to gain approval from before you begin to do what God has called you to do?

Many dreams and visions have been aborted because they were shared with the wrong people. These people seemed trustworthy, but they turned out to be abortionists who put in their knife of unbelief and killed the dream before it could be birthed. Be careful whom you share your cause of life with. Others can either kill it or nurture it. Look for those people who will nurture your vision, and avoid those who would kill it.

Now, let's look at what the Church sometimes calls *pride,* when, in reality, it is true humility, just the opposite of pride. I speak of someone taking God at His word and doing exactly what He says to do. Is that not what David was doing in this case? Why is it that when a person has simply taken God at His word, someone in the Church always has to call it pride? When we take God at His word, we're not working on presumption or assumption. We are working on His initiative and His delegated authority, which, in the end, He will confirm before the eyes of everyone.

Maybe we could now use Eliab's negative statement in a more positive way? God is looking for "arrogant," "insolent," and "rebellious" people, those who will set themselves against the standards of this world and all the initiatives of Satan (which are in direct opposition to God's Word). Be the one "rebellious" sister who believes that she should not be unequally yoked to an unbeliever. Be that one "arrogant" mother who believes God for her entire household to be saved. Be that one "strange" elderly person who believes God's promise (*"as thy days, so shall thy strength be,"* Deuteronomy 33:25).

God is looking for a child of His who is presently at the point of death but who will cry out and say as He has promised, *"I shall not die, but live, and declare the works of the Lord"* (Psalm 118:17). Until you are desperate enough to be "arrogant" and "rebellious" in the eyes of the world, Satan (and even many Christian believers), you are not a candidate to become *A Man [or Woman] After God's Own Heart.*

IS THERE NOT A CAUSE?

And David said. What have I now done? Is there not a cause?

This word *cause* as used here means *"covenant, word, promise, matter, thing, and lawsuit.* What is the Word of the Lord to you? What is the promise of God to you concerning your life, your ministry, your family and your nation? The moment the devil violates that word, he has entered into a legal battle with you. What he has done is a violation of your God-given right, and when taken to the throne of God for judgement, Satan will lose every legal battle against you, against your family, and against your ministry. Paul wrote:

And you who, being dead in your sins and in the uncircumcision of your flesh, hath he quickened together with him, having forgiven you all trespasses; blotting out the handwriting of ordinances that was against us, which was contrary to us, and took it out of the way, nailing it to his cross; and having spoiled principalities and powers, he made a show of them openly, triumphing over them in it.

Colossians 2:13-15

You have a cause for victory in the precious blood of Jesus Christ our Lord and Savior. Therefore know that you are covenanted with God for all things that pertains to life and godliness, as Peter taught us:

> *You are covenanted with God for all things that pertains to life and godliness!*

According as his divine power hath given unto us all things that pertain unto life and godliness, through the knowledge of him that hath called us to glory and virtue. Whereby are giving unto us exceeding great and precious promises: that by these ye might be partakers of his divine nature, having escaped the corruption that is in the world through lust.

2 Peter 1:3-4

Fight the good fight of faith and lay hold upon the course the Lord has set before you. Finish your course with all accuracy and at every cost. If you fall, rise again. Losing a battle does not mean losing the war. Be as Solomon, when he said:

69

For a just man falleth seven times, and riseth up again.
                                              Proverbs 24:16

Have a winning attitude, and fight for your cause. There are great and precious promises to be obtained. There is a divine nature to be partaken of, so escape from your lusts and move ahead unto victory, for nothing shall separate you from the love of God which is in Christ Jesus our Lord (see Romans 8:38-39).

If you can lay hold of the truth concerning your covenant with the Almighty, you are well on your way to becoming *A Man After God's Own Heart*.   ♥

CHAPTER 4

LEARNING TO INQUIRE OF GOD

A MAN AFTER GOD'S OWN HEART INQUIRES OF GOD CONCERNING HIS EVERY STEP.

And it came to pass, when Abiathar the son of Ahimelech fled to David in Keilah, that he came down with an ephod in his hand.

And David knew that Saul secretly practiced mischief against him; and he said to Abiathar the priest, Bring hither the ephod. Then said David, O LORD God of Israel, thy servant hath certainly heard that Saul seeketh to come to Keilah, to destroy the city for my sake. Will the men of Keilah deliver me up into his hand? Will Saul come down, as thy servant hath heard? O LORD God of Israel, I beseech thee, tell thy servant.

And the LORD said, He will come down.

Then said David, will the men of Keilah deliver me and my men into the hand of Saul?

And the LORD said, They will deliver thee up.

1 Samuel 23:6 and 9-12

David took it upon himself to always inquire of God concerning his every action and that of his men. He inquired of God not only concerning his military battles, about also about every pursuit in life. He wanted to know the end of a matter before he committed to it. This shows that he was indeed *A Man After God's Own Heart*. The Bible tells us:

The steps of a good man are ordered by the LORD.
                                    Psalm 37:23

Wise men always seek the counsel of the Lord because that is what will *"stand"*:

There are many devices in a man's heart; nevertheless the counsel of the Lord, that shall stand.
                                    Proverbs 19:21

We may have many imaginations flooding our minds, some of which are even suggestions from Satan himself. This happened to David when he was tempted to number Israel. We must take our imaginations and submit them to the counsel of the Lord. It is His counsel that will withstand the test of time. When our works are purged by fire in the last day, only that which has resulted from the counsel of the Lord will withstand the heat.

DAVID INQUIRED OF THE LORD IN HIS GRIEF

On another occasion, David inquired of the Lord in his grief:

And David inquired at the LORD, saying, Shall I pursue after this troop? Shall I overtake them?
And he answered him, Pursue: for thou shalt surely overtake them, and without fail recover all.

1 Samuel 30:8

In moments of great loss, grief, and distress, what should we do? Sometimes, like David and his men, it's only natural for us to weep and imagine the worst. But after you have grieved, please take time to inquire of God about the final outcome of the matter?

David was wise enough to do this and, as a result, a situation that seemed to be a total loss for him turned out to be gain. He pursued his enemies according to the word of the Lord, and he was able to overtake them and recover his losses. Then, he gained many spoils in the process.

> *Gather around you people of like precious faith who can labor with you in prayer until you recover all!*

After you have inquired of God concerning your matter and He tells you to pursue, gather around you people of like precious faith who can labor with you in prayer until you recover all. Some quite faint in the way, but there are those who will endure with you to the very end.

Don't forget to share your blessing with those who have labored with you, even those who only pursued with you halfway. Celebrate with your friends when God helps you to recover your losses. Throw them a victory party.

Jesus, in His parable of the lost coin and lost sheep explained:

And when he cometh home, he calleth together his friends and neighbours, saying unto them, Rejoice with me; for I have found my sheep which was lost.

Luke 15:6

INQUIRY CONCERNING BATTLE

Why do we need to inquire of the Lord more than once? Because His answer to the very same question is not always the same:

And David inquired of the LORD, saying, Shall I go up to the Philistines? wilt thou deliver them into mine hand?
And the LORD said unto David, Go up: for I will doubtless deliver the Philistines into thine hand.

2 Samuel 5:19

And when David inquired of the LORD, he said, Thou shalt not go up; but fetch a compass behind them, and come upon them over against the mulberry trees. And let it be, when thou hearest the sound of a going in the tops of the mulberry trees, that then thou shalt bestir

74

thyself: for then shall the LORD *go out before thee, to smite the host of the Philistines.*   2 Samuel 5:23-24

Here we see David inquiring of God on two different occasions concerning battle with the same enemy. On one occasion, God told him to go up, and on another occasion, the Lord told him not to go. The timing was not yet right.

You may be fighting the same enemy over and over again. You defeat him once, and expect to never see him again, but you'll not only see him again. This time, he'll be wiser, having learned something from his first defeat.

Anytime you face an enemy, inquire of God for the strategy needed to defeat him—even if it happens to be the very same enemy. God might want you to use another strategy this time. Thank God for the Holy Spirit whom we have today in our midst, guiding us into all truth:

Howbeit when he, the Spirit of truth, is come, he will guide you into all truth: for he shall not speak of himself; but whatsoever he shall hear, that shall he speak; and he will show you things to come.   John 16:13

This second account of David inquiring of God gives us a vivid picture of the Holy Spirit helping us in our battles and shows us our dependency on Him to help and guide us. We need to know when the Spirit of God in us wants to move, and then we need to stir ourselves to move with Him. In other words, we need to get into the flow of the Spirit of God and stay in that flow if we are to be successful in life and in ministry.

If we can make it our duty to inquire of God concerning our every move in life, we become more and more conscious of the Spirit's presence in our lives to lead and guide us, and, consequently, we will make fewer mistakes. Our lives, our family's lives, our jobs, our ministries, our careers, our sustenance and our establishment all depend on our ability to hear God's voice and our willingness to obey. Our lives depend on it, so never treat this need lightly.

At one point, when he was tempted to number Israel, David stopped inquiring of God, and the blessing ceased from him and his people. This one foolish and self-willed act led to the deaths of thousands of Israelis. Whatever our heavenly Father says to us we must do. The lives of many Christians have been sacrificed because of our lack of obedience. Learn to inquire of God, and you can quickly become *A Man After God's Own Heart.*   ♥

CHAPTER 5

RELATING YOUR COVENANT WITH GOD TO MAN

A MAN AFTER GOD'S OWN HEART EXTENDS HIS COVENANT WITH GOD TO HIS FELLOWMAN.

And it came to pass, when he had made an end of speaking unto Saul, that the soul of Jonathan was knit with the soul of David, and Jonathan loved him as his own soul. And Jonathan and David made a covenant, because he loved him as his own soul.

1 Samuel 18:1 & 3

It's wonderful to have a covenant with God, but being a man or woman after God's own heart requires that we extend this covenant to others around us as well.

We all enjoy the benefits of God's unconditional love, forgiveness, grace, favor and mercy. Sometimes we even demand it of Him and put Him in remembrance of His promises to us. But too often we forget that our Lord has called us to be like Him in this regard. He said:

Be ye therefore perfect, even as your Father which is in heaven is perfect. Matthew 5:48

And as ye would that men should do to you, do ye also to them likewise. Luke 6:31

If the Lord is calling us to be *"perfect"* and to do to others what we would have them do to us, this means that we need to treat others as God treats us. If we can demand God to demonstrate the loving nature of His covenant toward us, can we expect to get by with less when it comes to our treatment of our fellow man?

> **We need to treat others as God treats us!**

THE COVENANT BETWEEN JONATHAN AND DAVID

A wonderful example of covenant between men is found in this story of Saul and David. Jonathan, Saul's Son, and David were both men after God's heart, and they extended covenant to each other because they loved each other.

Covenant must always be entered into with a heart of love. In this case, the hearts of David and Jonathan were "knit" together in love, and it was out of this love that they extended to each other this covenant.

As a sign of the seriousness of the covenant into which they were entering, Jonathan stripped himself of his clothes and armor and gave them to David:

And Jonathan stripped himself of the robe that was

upon him, and gave it to David, and his garments,
even to his sword, and to his bow, and to his girdle.

1 Samuel 18:4

THE GIVING OF THE GARMENTS AND GIRDLE

Jonathan giving his garments to David tells us that the covenant between them was one of openness and transparency. There must be no secret between them and no shame. In that moment, they stood naked before each other, for they were there to act as a covering for each other. Between them, there would be absolute openness.

In keeping with this openness, Jonathan could not refrain himself from telling David of his father's evil intention toward him. After all, how could he be silent? He was in covenant with David, and covenant took precedence over his loyalty to his father.

The giving of the princely garments was also prophetic. By giving them to David, Jonathan was saying that he was giving up his right to the throne next of his father. David would be the next in line. Amazingly, Jonathan was not jealous of David's success, and neither was he competing with him for the throne. He was ready and willing to sacrifice it all for his friend.

This is extraordinary, and we need such a spirit among us today. If we walk in covenant with our brethren, we will not be in competition with them. We will rejoice in their successes and never be jealous of their blessings.

THE GIVING OF THE SWORD AND BOW

The giving of the sword and bow symbolized the fact that David and Jonathan would be there to protect each other. David would be Jonathan's defense, and Jonathan would be David's defense. They would defend each other and never strike out at each other. They would protect each other with their lives because they were in covenant together.

Later, when a man came claiming that he had killed Saul, David immediately commanded the young men around the man to slay him. When Ish-bosheth was slain by his servants and some came to David and told him about it, he ordered their death too because his covenant was not only with Jonathan, but also with his family. Having taken Jonathan's sword and bow, David was an avenger of blood for Jonathan and his immediate family.

THE CASE OF MEPHIBOSHETH

After Saul and Jonathan were dead and David had become king, he sought for someone from the house of Saul to whom he could show kindness *"for Jonathan's sake"*:

And the king said, Is there not any of the house of Saul, that I may show the kindness of God unto him? And Ziba said unto the king, Jonathan hath yet a son, which is lame on his feet.
And the King said unto him, Where is he? And Ziba said unto the king, Behold, he is in the house of Machir, the son of Ammiel, in Lo-de-bar.

2 Samuel 9:3-4

The man in question, Mephibosheth, was immediately sent for.

Now this Mephibosheth had been a very unfortunate person to this point. When he was still a child, his grandfather lost the throne. As his nurse carried him away to safety, he was dropped, and this caused him to become lame.

Grandson of a former king, Mephibosheth was now lame and living in what was known as a pastureless land. He had been forgotten by the vast multitude of the people, and had received none of the possessions of his grandfather. In his sad condition, he didn't even have anyone to show him pity or kindness.

Isn't this is the plight of many today? Some have vowed to their friends, now dead, to take care of their children. But, not only have they not met the children's immediate needs. They have actually stolen the children's inheritance, using their dead friend's children for their own gain. That's what men of the world are like.

David was different! His heart cried for any who were left of Saul's house, for he longed to show them some kindness. He did not betray his friend's trust. Those who are called "friends" today all too often wind up stealing a man's wife and children from him. What a betrayal of trust! David was a covenant man, and a covenant man would never do that.

Now when Mephibosheth, the son of Jonathan, the son of Saul, was come unto David, he fell on his face, and did reverence. And David said, Mephibosheth. And he answered, behold thy servant!

81

And David said unto him, Fear not: for I will surely show thee kindness for Jonathan thy father's sake, and will restore thee all the lands of Saul thy father; and thou shalt eat bread at my table continually.
And he bowed himself, and said, What is thy servant, that thou shouldest look upon such a dead dog as I am?   1 Samuel 9:6-8

The fact that David's heart cried to show the kindness of the Lord to any of Saul's house *"for Jonathan's sake,"* because of the covenant he had made with him, is clearly not normal in our world. This "kindness" he wanted to demonstrate was not a kindness of his own, the kindness of a man; it was the kindness of the Lord.

David knew that Mephibosheth was no threat to him. He had not taken the throne of Saul of his own will; it had been God's gift to him. He knew the truth, that it is God who exalts a man and God who puts a man down.

He removeth kings, and setteth up kings; he giveth wisdom unto the wise, and knowledge to them that know understanding.   Daniel 2:21

David made no attempt to secure his position by killing his enemies, as many do. Instead, he showed kindness to them, understanding that his security came from God.

All that mattered to David now was his covenant with Jonathan. Jonathan had not felt threatened by David and had showed him kindness. Why should Mephibosheth now threaten be a threat to David? Jonathan did not secured his position, so why should David secure his?

God took David from caring for the sheep and made him king over Israel. And, in the same way, David now took Mephibosheth from a pastureless land, restored to him the lands of his father, and brought him to live in Jerusalem, to sit at his table and eat with him, just like one of his sons. A man after God's own heart will demonstrate to others the same kindness God has demonstrated to him.

HAVE WE FORGOTTEN?

Some of us have forgotten where God brought us from and the mercy He showed to us. We've forgotten how much we struggled to be His child, and now we're the first to cast stones at others. Some of us have been guilty of the very same offenses, only our sins have never been exposed. How can we afford to show others mercy, when we need it so much ourselves? Jesus said:

> *This "kindness" David wanted to demonstrate was not a kindness of his own; it was the kindness of the Lord!*

He that is without sin among you, let him first cast a stone at her.   John 8:7

Shouldest not thou also have had compassion on thy fellow servant, even as I had pity on thee.

Matthew 18:33

When famine overran the land for a period of three years, David asked the Lord why, and He said that it was because Saul had treated the Gibeonites so poorly, slaying them mercilessly, although Israel had historically maintained a covenant with them. David called the leaders of the Gibeonites to come to him, and when they had come he asked them what atonement he could make to satisfy the grievances of their people.

The Gibeonites refused all offers of gold and silver and said they would only be satisfied if seven of Saul's descendants were handed over to them to be publicly hanged. David reluctantly agreed, and Mephibosheth should have been at the top of the list. But, for Jonathan's sake, David found suitable substitutes, and Mephibosheth was again spared:

But the king spared Mephibosheth, the son of Jonathan the son of Saul, because of the Lord's oath that was between them, between David and Jonathan the son of Saul.

2 Samuel 21:7

David was indeed *A Man After God's Own Heart*.

COVENANT BROTHERHOOD

I'm afraid that what is lacking among many today in

Christendom is what I have come to call "covenant brotherhood." This is what David and Jonathan had. Covenant brotherhood means that we seek each other's interests, rather than our own.

If you win in battle, I will rejoice with you. If you fall in battle, I will mourn for you, compose a poem or sing a song in your memory and not criticize you anymore. If you die, I will take care of your wife and children.

In many parts of the world, the residence of certain communities have banned together to develop neighborhood watch groups. These groups patrol the neighborhoods, thus protecting each other's homes and businesses. We Christians need to form such a group among fellow pastors and ministers. Jesus said:

> *By this shall all men know that ye are my disciples, if*
> *ye have love one to another.*   John 13:35

The man who has received God's love and extended covenant to others because of that love has made great strides toward becoming *A Man After God's Own Heart.*♥

85

CHAPTER 6

LEARNING NOT TO AVENGE YOURSELF OF YOUR ENEMIES

A MAN AFTER GOD'S OWN HEART DOES NOT AVENGE HIMSELF OF HIS ENEMIES. INSTEAD, HE LEAVES THEM IN THE HANDS OF GOD. WHEN GOD JUDGES HIS ENEMIES, HE MOURNS FOR THEM.

And David said to Abishai, Destroy him not: for who can stretch forth his hand against the LORD's anointed, and be guiltless?   1 Samuel 26:9

WHO SHALL TOUCH THE LORD'S ANOINTED AND REMAIN GUILTLESS?

When David first appeared on the scene, Saul was happy to receive him. In time, however, Saul turned against David and pursued him with the intent of killing him, all because he thought David had become a threat to his throne. He confessed to Jonathan, his son, that as long as David was alive there could be no future for him.

When a lull came in the battles Israel was fighting against her enemies, Saul took the opportunity to go after his perceived rival. He followed David into the rocks where the wild goats roamed, and when he grew weary, he went into a cave to rest. As it happened, David and his men were hiding nearby:

> *And the men of David said unto him, Behold the day of which the LORD said unto thee, Behold I will deliver thine enemy into thine hand, that thou mayest do to him as it shall seem good unto thee.*
> *Then David rose, and cut off the skirt of Saul's robe privily. And it came to pass afterward, that David's heart smote him, because he had cut off Saul's skirt. And he said unto his men, The LORD forbid that I should do this thing unto my master, the LORD's anointed, to stretch forth mine hand against him, seeing he is the anointed of the LORD. So David stayed his servants with these words, and suffered them not to rise against Saul. But Saul rose up out of the cave, and went on his way.*
>
> 1 Samuel 24:4-7

I've never read anywhere in the Scriptures where it was previously prophesied concerning David the words his men uttered on that day: *"Behold the day of which the Lord said unto thee, Behold I will deliver thine enemy into thine hand, that thou mayest do to him as it shall seem good unto thee."* It appears that someone was prophesying to David, and what they were prophesying did not agree with the Word of God.

David knew the heart of God, who said:

> *Touch not mine anointed, and do my prophets no harm.*
>
> Psalm 105:15

To me belongeth vengeance and recompence.

Deuteronomy 32:35

David chose to put more weight in what God thought than in what men thought.

What would happen if God actually said to us to do to our enemies what seemed good to us? What might we do? Would we be merciful to them? Or would we utterly destroy them?

Unlike Saul, David had control of his men. He was not swayed by their opinions, nor did he allow them to do whatever they felt like doing. His heart convicted him even for cutting off Saul's robe, so he refrained himself and his men from doing any further damage to this enemy.

What motivated David to spare Saul? He could not help but recognize the anointing upon Saul's life. God had set this man up as head over Israel. This caused David to respect Saul, even when it seemed that Saul was not worthy of respect. Saul was God's servant, and if he required discipline, then that discipline must come at the hand of God Himself, not at David's hand.

David later said to Saul:

> *David chose to put more weight in what God thought than in what men thought!*

The LORD judge between me and thee, and the LORD avenge me of thee: but mine hand shall not be upon thee. 1 Samuel 24:12

Some of us are guilty of attempting to avenge ourselves of our enemies. We may not always do it directly, but we do nothing to prevent those around us from doing the damage. David not only refused to do it himself; he also stayed the hands of others who wanted to do it for him. This demonstrated that he was a man after God's own heart.

JESUS' TEACHINGS ON VENGEANCE

Jesus showed us the Father's will in this regard:

Then said Jesus unto him, Put up again thy sword into his place: for all they that take the sword shall perish with the sword. Thinkest thou that I cannot now pray to my Father, and he shall presently give me more than twelve legions of angels? Matthew 26:52-53

When faced with the ultimate sacrifice, our Lord prayed:

Father forgive them; for they know not what they do. Luke 23:34

Not one word of vengeance was heard from Him.

What is your attitude toward those who falsely judge you, criticize you, and give you a bad name? What should it be? First, you must do as Jesus did, learn to pray for your enemies. The more you pray for them, the less you'll be tempted to avenge yourself of them. When you pray for them, God will do the avenging.

I've been in the ministry long enough now to see people who did me wrong in the past coming back on bended knee to confess their wrong, say they're sorry, and ask for my forgiveness. Fortunately, God taught me to pray for such people long ago. When I met them anywhere, I was always led to greet them. Sometimes, I was even led to send them gifts. This was true even of some who had shouted abuses at me and called me a hypocrite.

David, time and time again, showed that this was his constant attitude—not to avenge himself of his enemies, but to leave all judgment in the hands of God. For example, later on David had yet another opportunity to kill Saul. His companion on this occasion, a man named Abishai, considered this to be a perfect opportunity and encouraged David to take it, to kill the king or allow him to do it. Again David refused:

> *And David said to Abishai, Destroy him not: for who can stretch forth his hand against the LORD's anointed, and be guiltless?* 1 Samuel 26:9

Taking Saul's spear and his water canister was as far as David allowed himself to go on this occasion. This would speak to Saul and show him that his life had again been spared.

There is a very important lesson to be learned here. Anyone who decides to become the judge of one of

God's servants and condemns them (even when they may be in a backslidden state, as Saul clearly was) will not remain guiltless. Paul confirmed this by saying:

Who art thou that judgest another man's servant? to his own master he standeth or falleth. Yea, he shall be holden up: for God is able to make him stand.

Romans 14:4

> **A man after God's own heart weeps when his enemy is judged!**

If this is true even of *"another man's servant,"* how much more so of God's servant?

And this truth holds even in extreme cases. It really doesn't matter if you're being abused and taken advantage of by a minister under whom you're currently serving. Serve in that capacity faithfully until the Lord shows you to move on to some other task. Never be guilty of engaging in a plotted coup or a conspiracy against a man or woman of God. Never be guilty of slandering or backbiting them. If you do this, you cannot be held guiltless.

If it's time for you to leave a ministry you've not been happy with, leave with just what is yours. Don't be guilty of splitting the congregation. Pleasing God is more important than any other concern.

David didn't take the kingdom from Saul by force. After Saul died, the people of Israel sought David out and crowned him king over them. God knows how to elevate you, so let Him do it in His own way and in His own time, never taking things into your own hands.

WEEPING WHEN YOUR ENEMY IS JUDGED

As we noted at the outset, a man after God's own heart weeps when his enemy is judged. When Saul died, David wept and mourned for him. He even went so far as to order the death of an Amalekite who professed to have help the king die.

Some of Saul's descendants continued to fight against David, but David grew stronger, and they grew weaker (see 2 Chronicles 3:1). As we noted earlier in this chapter, one day a group of men took it upon themselves to kill Saul's son Ishbosheth. They brought his head to David, thinking that he would give them a reward. Instead, David was angry with them:

> When one told me, saying, Behold, Saul is dead, thinking to have brought good tidings, I took hold of him, and slew him in Ziklag, who thought that I would have given him a reward for his tidings: how much more, when wicked men have slain a righteous person in his own house upon his bed? Shall I not therefore now require his blood of your hand, and take you away from the earth?
>
> 2 Samuel 4:10-11

These men who had killed Isbosheth were, in turn, killed, and their dead bodies were publicly displayed for all to see. The head of Ishbosheth, son of Saul, was buried honorably.

Then there was Abner, son of Saul's cousin, Ner, and captain over Saul's army. He took Ishbosheth and made him king instead of David. When Joab, David's longtime and faithful aide, killed Abner, thinking that he had done David a great favor, David, instead, mourned for Abner and even declared a curse upon Joab and his family for having killed him.

We must learn that there will always be adversaries or opposition in life, and not everyone whom you see as an adversary is evil. Just because someone disagrees with you doesn't make them evil. Others surely see *you* as an adversary, and you don't consider yourself to be evil, do you? Should you kill everyone who disagrees with you?

As you go through life, there will always be those who don't think like you do or see things from the same perspective. That's just the way life is. When one of these "enemies" dies, will you be thankful, or will you wish you had found a way to be their friend? Will you remember only the bad things they did or said to you, or will you choose to concentrate on the good they've done in life?

What is God's will regarding even evil people? Is it not that they be freed from their evil to glorify Him? Rebuke the evil spirits in them, and help them to be free to praise and glorify God.

YOU ARE SECURE IN GOD

What are you so worried about? Does the Bible not promise you:

No weapon that is formed against thee shall prosper;

and every tongue that shall rise against thee in judg-
ment thou shalt condemn. This is the heritage of the
servants of the LORD, and their righteousness is of me,
saith the LORD.   Isaiah 54:17

Behold, I give unto you power to tread on serpents and
scorpions, and over all the power of the enemy: and
nothing shall by any means hurt you.   Luke 10:19

You have nothing to fear, so don't despise those who simply disagree with you.

Why is it that pastors need to send spies to dig up some dirt against each other? What a shame! Some are looking forward to the fall of the other instead of believing and praying for their exaltation. Brothers and sisters, we're all on the same team, and the Kingdom of God is not some personality contest called Empire Building.

No! We're all one Body, and we need each other. We're here to complement each other and not to compete with each other.

Jesus taught us to love even our enemies:

Ye have heard that it hath been said, Thou shalt love
thy neighbour, and hate thy enemy. But I say unto
you, Love your enemies, bless them that curse you, do
good to them that hate you, and pray for them which
despitefully use you, and persecute you; that ye may
be the children of your Father which is in heaven: for
he maketh his sun to rise on the evil and on the good,
and sendeth rain on the just and on the unjust.
                                    Matthew 5:43-45

It was then, in verse 48, in relationship to our attitude toward others, that Jesus spoke of us being *"perfect"* as He is perfect. Surely we all have a long way to go to achieve this targeted perfection.

A Lamentation for Saul

The mourning song that came forth from David's heart upon the death of Saul is beautiful and challenging:

The beauty of Israel is slain upon thy high places: how are the mighty fallen!

Tell it not in Gath, publish it not in the streets of Askelon; lest the daughters of the Philistines rejoice, lest the daughters of the uncircumcised triumph.

Ye mountains of Gilboa, let there be no dew, neither let there be rain, upon you, nor fields of offerings: for there the shield of the mighty is vilely cast away, the shield of Saul, as though he had not been anointed with oil.

From the blood of the slain, from the fat of the mighty, the bow of Jonathan turned not back, and the sword of Saul returned not empty.

Saul and Jonathan were lovely and pleasant in their lives, and in their death they were not divided: they were swifter than eagles, they were stronger than lions.

Ye daughters of Israel, weep over Saul, who clothed you in scarlet, with other delights, who put on ornaments of gold upon your apparel.

How are the mighty fallen in the midst of the battle!

2 Samuel 1:19-25

This is how a real man mourns for his enemies, and this is the attitude that makes him a man after God's own heart. In this moment, David did not remember Saul's wrongdoings, but rather his goodness. He did not remember Saul's weaknesses, but rather his strengths. He did not want Saul's enemies to rejoice at his death. That would be a shame.

How can we adopt such an attitude? By remembering our own failings and the Lord's mercy toward us:

> *God commendeth his love toward us, in that, while we were yet sinners, Christ died for us.*
>
> Romans 5:8

> *In this moment, David did not remember Saul's wrongdoings, but rather his goodness!*

As He has shown us compassion, let us extend compassion to others, even our enemies, real or imagined. You need not avenge yourself of any wrongdoing in this life. God will do it for you. Understanding that truth can go a long way toward making you *A Man After God's Own Heart.* ♥

CHAPTER 7

BEING WILLING TO CONFESS AND FORSAKE YOUR SINS

A MAN AFTER GOD'S OWN HEART ACKNOWLEDGES AND TAKES RE-SPONSIBILITY FOR HIS SINS, AND HE FORSAKES THEM.

I acknowledge my transgressions: and my sin is ever before me.   Psalm 51:3

As we have seen, Saul always made excuses for his sin. Until the very last minutes of his life, he was still blaming his failures on others. For instance, he knew that his pursuit of David was wrong, but he did it anyway.

SOMEONE MUST TAKE RESPONSIBILITY

Leaders must take responsibility for their actions. Whatever they allow or disallow, whether it has been their idea or someone else's, they are responsible. They always have the last word.

In marriage, I believe that the final decision should always rest with the husband. I don't believe that any

After a leader has weighed all the input from his associates, it's then up to him to make a decision, and to bear the responsibility for whatever decision he makes!

husband should make a decision without first consulting with his wife. But whether a given suggestion has been the wife's or the husband's, he must take responsibility for it.

In a church setting or even a business setting, after a leader has weighed all the input from his associates, it's then up to him to make a decision, and he alone must bear the responsibility for whatever decision he makes.

In both victory or defeat, we are responsible. We are usually careful to take the credit for a job well done, but we should also be ready to assume the blame when things do not go well. The great German evangelist Reinhardt Bonnke is reported to have said that he will give God the glory for every person who is healed in his crusades, but that he will personally take the blame for anyone who is not. That's the attitude of a real leader!

As we noted in a previous chapter, Adam blamed Eve for

his failures, just like many husbands do today. Most Christians have the habit of blaming everything on Satan, but Satan only makes suggestions. We always have to power to act or not to act. Therefore we are responsible for our actions, not Satan.

DAVID AND SIN

On two separate occasions, David was confronted by someone who made up a story, seemingly telling what someone else had done, but in actuality illustrating his failings. When he pronounced the parties guilty and ordered them to be punished, he didn't realize that *he* was actually the guilty party. When he was told outright that he was the man, however, he readily and willingly repented of his sins and made the necessary amends.

Just because you're a man or woman of God doesn't mean that you'll no longer sin or make mistakes. But what makes you a real man or woman of God is your willingness to acknowledge, confess, and forsake your sins and face whatever consequence may follow. If we can boldly confess our righteous deeds, we should also be ready and willing to confess our failings.

David, for instance, acknowledged and confessed his wrongdoing after his adultery with Bath-sheba:

Have mercy upon me, O God, according to thy lovingkindness: according unto the multitude of thy tender mercies blot out my transgressions.
Wash me throughly from mine iniquity, and cleanse me from my sin.

101

*For I ACKNOWLEDGE my transgressions: and my
sin is ever before me.*   Psalm 51:1-3

David was not perfect, but he was always quick to
confess his imperfections. Because of this, he not only
experienced God's grace for victory; he also experienced
God's grace to forgive his sins. God has made provision
for both these types of grace, for He knows that we are
but flesh, and therefore we will sin. He knows that there
are times when we will yield to the suggestions of the
world, the flesh, and the devil, and so He has already
made provision for those moment. His Word declares:

*My little children, these things write I unto you, that ye
sin not. And if any man sin, we have an advocate with
the Father, Jesus Christ the righteous: and he is the propi-
tiation for our sins: and not for ours only, but also for the
sins of the whole world.*   1 John 2:1-2

A life of sinlessness is our goal, our ideal, but when
we fail to hit the mark, we know where to turn for forgiveness.

THE APOSTLE PAUL EXPERIENCED WEAKNESS

Paul, as great an apostle as he was, spoke of *"infirmities,"* and *"reproaches,"* and of being *"weak"*:
*Therefore I take pleasure in infirmities, in reproaches,
in necessities, in persecutions, in distresses for Christ's
sake: for when I am weak then I am strong.*
                    2 Corinthians 12:10

Most of us make the mistake of trying to hide any weaknesses that we have and of trying to gloss over any and all failings, thinking that this is necessary if we are to maintain the respect of others. But if Paul had weak moments, then we can expect to have them too. None of us is perfect, and each of us is human—leaders at every level included. When we inevitably fail, the important thing is to recognize that failure as quickly as possible, seek God's forgiveness for it, and, at the same time, seek His strength not to repeat the same mistake again. When we do that, our weaknesses turn to strengths, and we are on the road to becoming *A Man After God's Own Heart*.

THE SCRIPTURES MAKE NO EFFORT TO HIDE DAVID'S SIN

Because David was said to be *"a man after his [God's] own heart,"* some mistakenly think that he must have been perfect. A cursory reading of the Scriptures disproves this foolish thinking. The Scriptures do nothing to hide the man's faults. Two particular sins of David are the most remembered: (1) He committed adultery with Bath-sheba, and (2) He numbered Israel contrary to God's command. But there were others. He said, *"My sin is ever before me."* And still he was *A Man After God's Own Heart.*

These two sins, in particular, were grievous and adversely affected the lives of many people. And yet, despite these flagrant failings and the consequences he (and the people) suffered because of them, David picked himself up and went on to serve God and be the best king he could be. Looking back now at the overall picture, it is clear that his life characterized Christ and came as close to the express image of the Father as any of us can dare to come—despite every failing.

Some may well object to this personal assessment, asking, "How can a person sin and still be a man or woman after God's own heart?" I understand where they're coming from, but today, in the age of grace, with the born-again experience available to us and the indwelling of the Holy Spirit encouraged for every believer, Christians are still not perfect. Their failures are clearly visible to everyone around them. So if we believe that we must be perfect, as man counts perfection, to make it to Heaven, none of us will qualify.

We all do sin, and it is by grace that we stand day by day. Still, in the midst of their personal failures, we can be constantly moving forward in service to God. Having faults did not prevent David from becoming a man who pleased God, and your faults need not keep you from His best for your life either.

In many ways, David was a type of Christ. He was, for example, the only king who operated in the offices of king, prophet, and priest. Saul tried it, and it didn't work for him. David was somehow different. He received such favor from God that the Almighty Himself swore an oath that until Christ came there would always be a descendant of David on the throne of Israel.

This oath was challenged while David was still alive. Twice, others revolted against him and tried to overthrow him, but both times he was able to maintain his throne. It was truly established forever. What a success story!

Success does not mean the absence of troubles and failures along our journey. It means victory despite every trouble and failure, and David rejoiced in that kind of victory.

> *Success does not mean the absence of troubles and failures along our journey!*

DAVID KNEW HOW TO TREAT SIN AND YOU MUST TOO

If a man sins, that does not necessarily make him a sinner. It is when a man *practices* sin that he becomes a sinner. If a man gets up from his sin, make amends, and continues in righteousness, then he is not a sinner at all. He is a righteous man.

David was wise enough to know that he must confess and forsake his sins, not cover them. He understood the scriptural truth:

> *He that covereth his sins shall not prosper: but whoso confesseth and forsaketh them shall have mercy.*
> Proverbs 28:13

We cannot say that David was without sin, but we can say that he was a man of mercy. He made it so by his willingness to face his personal weaknesses and overcome them. This will make any man *A Man After God's Own Heart*. ♥

CHAPTER 8

DETERMINING TO
BUILD GOD'S HOUSE

A MAN AFTER GOD'S OWN HEART DEDICATES HIMSELF TO BUILD
GOD'S HOUSE.

*And it came to pass, when the king sat in his house,
and the LORD had given him rest round about from all
his enemies; that the king said unto Nathan the prophet,
See now, I dwell in an house of cedar, but the ark of
God dwelleth within curtains. And Nathan said to the
king, Go, do all that is in thine heart; for the LORD is
with thee.*   2 Samuel 7:1-3

There are so many great things to remember about
David that it is impossible to cover them all in this one
volume. One of the greatest, of course, was David's burden to build God a house. How could he dwell in a lovely
house of cedar when God's presence, represented by the
Ark of the Covenant, was kept in a tent? It must not be.
He would build God a suitable house.

Before we get to that great story, however, let's look briefly at several other important points about David.

David As Revelator

To my way of thinking, the thing that crowned David's reign as Israel's greatest king was his ability to receive revelation from God. He was not only a king; he was also a true prophet of God. He contributed to the building of the Kingdom of God in every generation that followed him through the abundance of the revelations he left behind.

Peter, when preaching on the Day of Pentecost, recalled:

> *Men and brethren, let me freely speak unto you of the patriarch David, that he is both dead and buried, and his sepulchre is with us unto this day. Therefore being a prophet, and knowing that God had sworn with an oath to him, that of the fruit of his loins, according to the flesh, he would raise up Christ to sit on his throne; he seeing this before spake of the resurrection of Christ.*
>
> Acts 2:29-31

He then quoted from David in the Psalms.

What are some of the other things David foresaw in the Spirit?

In the Spirit, David foresaw the cessation of burnt offerings and sacrifices for the remission of sins:

Sacrifice and offering thou didst not desire; mine ears hast thou opened: burnt offering and sin offering hast thou not required.

Then said I, Lo I come: in the volume of the book as it is written of me.

Psalm 40:6-7

In the Spirit, David foresaw a kingdom of priests. He knew that the answer for his people was spiritual, not governmental:

And David built there an altar unto the Lord, and offered burnt offerings and peace offerings. So the LORD was entreated for the land, and the plague was stayed from Israel.

2 Samuel 24:25

In the Spirit, David foresaw the death, burial, and resurrection of Christ:

> **The thing that crowned David's reign as Israel's greatest king was his ability to receive revelation from God!**

The kings of the earth set themselves, and the rulers take counsel together, against the LORD, and against his anointed, saying, Let us break his bands asunder, and cast away their cords from us.

Psalm 2:2-3

*He seeing this before spake of the resurrection of Christ,
that his soul was not left in hell, neither his flesh did
see corruption.*   Acts 2:31

In the Spirit, David foresaw the Kingdom of God established on earth:

*O let the nations be glad and sing for joy: for thou
shalt judge the people righteously, and govern the nations upon the earth.*   Psalm 67:4

These and other great revelations contained in the psalms of David have blessed believers of every generation.

David As the Great Psalmist and Example of Worship

The psalms themselves were a substantial contribution to be used by the Body of Christ in our worship to God. David himself was a true worshipper, and his collection of powerful psalms are used today not only as songs, but also as meditations. They are used collectively, and they are used individually. What a blessing they have been to the Body of Christ!

David's Priestly Arrangements

David made another great contribution to the Kingdom of God in his order of worship:

And he appointed, ACCORDING TO THE ORDER OF DAVID HIS FATHER, the courses of the priests to their service, and the Levites to their charges, to praise and minister before the priests, as the duty of everyday required: the porters also by their courses at every gate: for so had David the man of God commanded.

2 Chronicles 8:14

David was the inspiration of the priestly arrangements that Solomon later instituted in the Temple he built. Solomon was blessed to put it all into practice, but it was actually David who arranged the patterns of service for the priests, Levites and porters. He left detailed orders with Solomon for what was to be done later. What a man of God he was! Oh, that each of us might find our place in the Body and make our special contribution, becoming *A Man After God's Own Heart.*

Do All That Is in Thine Heart; for the Lord Is With Thee

When David received the burden to build God's house, Nathan the prophet did not argue with him in the least. He had noticed that David had prophetic gifts himself and that the Spirit of God often inspired him. He suggested that David do just what was in his heart. Since God was with him, what was in his heart would, most likely, be pleasing to God.

In this case, it was not to be. God sent Nathan back later to say that David would not be permitted to build God a house because he had been a man of war. The honor of building a house for Him would go, instead, to David's son Solomon. There's an important principle to be learned here.

Those of us who love the Lord have His Spirit within us, and He often implants certain desires within us. We sometimes wake up in the morning, for instance, with a desire to bless a certain person or to do some particular good deed. We can't explain it; we just know that we have a sudden desire to do it.

> *God's Spirit often implants certain desires within us!*

We may want to somehow bless a certain work or a certain minister, to feed the poor, or to do something else useful in the Kingdom. When this happens, we often are surprised and don't know what to do. Nathan had the answer: do what the Spirit has placed in your heart. What David was to learn (even though he was not able to build God's house as he wanted) is that when we are willing to dedicate ourselves to building God's house, He will build ours. So when you become a missionary-supporting, vision-building, church-developing man or woman, then God will build your life and work and cause it to be established.

Many people are afraid to do what is in their hearts. Can they trust what they feel? They're not sure. Some go the extreme of asking God about every detail of life, what particular clothes they should put on that day, what foods they should eat. But God trusts you, and you can learn to trust yourself. He wants you to do what is in your heart to do, and He will bless it. It was born of His Spirit and then implanted into your spirit.

Yes, God has predetermined everything about your life. Paul, preaching in Athens, declared:

God that made the world and all things therein, seeing that He is Lord of heaven and earth, dwelleth not in temples made with hands; neither is worshipped with men's hands, as though he needed any thing, seeing he giveth to all life, and breath, and all things; and hath made of one blood all nations of men for to dwell on all the face of the earth, and hath determined the times before appointed, and the bounds of their habitation. Acts 17:24-26

It is all determined. Now, the Lord wants to implant a desire for it into your spirit, and then He wants you to do what is in your heart to do.

Everything has been predetermined since before the foundations of the world. God knows where you should start, and He also knows where you will end. He knows your successors, even before you choose them. Let His Spirit give you confidence that what is in your heart has been planted there by divine decree. Then, determine to do it.

But David's case was a little different. Why did he foresee the Temple in Jerusalem and have a burden to build it and yet God didn't allow him to do it? Did God somehow make a mistake? Of course not!

One thing is sure: David wanted to do it. But there are some things that God has not ordained for one generation, but for the next. We may be allowed to foresee it and even to make preparation for it and still not be allowed to enter into it. This is God's choice, so we need not pretend that we have done it. Like David, we can graciously make provision for what is to come and then hand the whole affair over to the capable hands of the next generation, having done our part.

God has not only determined our time and place of birth; He has also determined our spiritual boundaries. Trust Him, and do what He gives you to do—no more and no less.

"I WILL BUILD YOU A HOUSE"

David surely wanted to build God a house, but God said no. He wanted to build David a house instead:

Now therefore so shalt thou [Nathan] say to my servant David, Thus saith the LORD of Hosts, I took thee from the sheepcote, from following the sheep, to be ruler over my people, over Israel: and I was with thee whithersoever thou wentest, and have cut off all thine enemies out of thy sight, and have made thee a great name, like unto the name of the great men that are in the earth. Moreover I will appoint for my people Israel, and will plant them, that they may dwell in a place of their own, and move no more; neither shall the children of wickedness afflict them any more, as beforetime, and as since the time I commanded judges to be over my people Israel, and have caused thee to rest from all thine enemies. Also the LORD *telleth thee THAT HE WILL MAKE THEE AN HOUSE.*

And when thy days be fulfilled, and thou shalt sleep with thy fathers, I will set up THY SEED AFTER THEE, which will proceed out of thy bowels, AND I WILL ESTABLISH HIS KINGDOM. He shall build an house for my name, and I will establish the throne of his kingdom for ever. I will be his father, and he shall be my son. If he commit iniquity, I will chastise him with the rod of men, and with the stripes of the children of men: but my mercy shall not depart away from him, as I took it from Saul, whom I put away before thee. And THINE HOUSE AND THY KINGDOM SHALL BE ESTABLISHED FOR EVER before thee: thy throne shall be established for ever.

2 Samuel 7:8-16

God had given the people rest. They no longer lived in tents; they had settled in the land and had permanent dwellings. Tents were for pilgrims and strangers, and they typified movement. The people of Israel were home now, and God had granted them safety and prosperity in the land.

In all of this, David rejoiced. But still, he could not be happy. God was yet living in a tent, and that bothered David. It was time for God's house to be built. A foundation must be laid so that God could have a permanent dwelling place among His people. Thus, it came to David's heart to build God a house.

And because he desired it, even though he was not able to physically complete it, God honored his desire and decided to build His servant a house. His throne would be established forever.

The is just one of the many rewards that come through the law of sowing and reaping. Jesus declared:

Give, and it shall be given unto you; good measure, pressed down, and shaken together, and running over, shall men give into your bosom. For with the same measure that ye mete withal it shall be measured to you again. Luke 6:38

Paul taught emphatically:

Whatever a man sows, that he will also reap. Galatians 6:7

David sought to build God a house, and instead God built him a house. How wonderful!

What Was This "House" that God Built for David?

But what does the word *"house"* mean in this context? According to *Strong's,* it means "continuity and establishment." God told David that because of his faithfulness there would never cease to be a king from among his descendants to succeed him on the throne. God's mercy would never cease over David's house. If his sons were ungodly, then God would use other men to chastise them, but David's kingdom would continue until it was established in Christ. What an extraordinary promise for an extraordinary man!

MICHAL'S LOSS

One prominent person in this story did not share in David's glory. She was Michal, daughter of Saul and David's wife. She despised the man after God's own heart and, as a result, she became barren:

Because David desired to build God a house, God honored his desire and built His servant a house!

> *And David danced before the LORD with all his might; and David was girded with a linen ephod. So David and all the house of Israel brought up the ark of the LORD with shouting and with the sound of the trumpet. And the ark of the LORD came into the city of David, Michal Saul's daughter looked through a window, and saw king David leaping and dancing before the LORD; and SHE DESPISED HIM IN HER HEART.*
> *Then David returned to bless his household. And Michal the daughter of Saul came out to meet David,*

and said, How glorious was the king of Israel today, who uncovered himself today in the eyes of the handmaids of his servants, as one of the vain fellows, shamelessly uncovereth himself!

Therefore Michal the daughter of Saul had no child unto the day of her death.

2 Samuel 6:14-16, 20 and 23

Michal was a profile in tragedy. After she had been given to David in marriage, her father relented and gave her to another man. By this man, she gave birth to four children. But those children all died to stop the plague that had come upon Israel as a result of the sins of Saul. With David, the man of God, she had no children, because God shut up her womb. And this very passage of the sacred Scriptures shows us why.

Michal not only despised David in her heart when he danced before the Lord; she also confronted him about it, rebuking him and telling him that he had behaved like a vile and shameless person. The result was that Michal became unfruitful. She could no longer produce because she despised the worship of the Lord and him who loved the Lord so passionately.

I'm sure that Michal was not in favor of David's plan to build the house of the Lord. Why waste money on something like that? There were more urgent needs.

This barrenness of soul was now reflected in the barrenness of her flesh. She would bear no more seed. She would not experience continuity and establishment. She had no burden for God's house, for His worship, for the upbuilding of His Kingdom.

Oh Friend, I urge you today: don't be a Michal; be a David.

DAVID'S HEART

David's answer to Michal shows his heart:

And David said unto Michal, It was before the LORD, which chose me before thy father, and before all his house, to appoint me ruler over the people of the LORD, over Israel: therefore will I play before the LORD. And I will yet be more vile than thus, and will be base in mine own sight: and of the maidservants which thou hast spoken of, of them shall I be had in honour.

2 Samuel 6:21-22

When we're in the presence of the Lord, let's keep our dignity in our pockets and worship God freely.

Too often we ministers are those who insist on maintaining "dignity" in the House of God, refusing to worship and to praise God in the midst of the congregation and to encourage others to do the same. It's time that we abandoned this false dignity and began to dance before the Lord like David danced. We must be examples of true worship and praise before our people, and in so doing, we can inspire them to enter further into God's presence. We will all then experience the rain of God's glory in our midst. That's what a man after God's own heart does. Let's concentrate on building His house in the Spirit, and He will establish us.

What Will Your Contribution Be?

What will be your contribution toward building the Body of Christ on Earth? Whatever God has called you to contribute—songs, poems, books, finances, organizational ability—it's time to make your contribution. Ask the Lord what it is that you're to leave for the Body before you pass from the scene or before you move on to some other place. Whatever you do, don't go to your grave with your gift still unreleased. Do as Jesus taught:

> *Ask the Lord what it is that you're to leave for the Body!*

Let your light so shine before men, that they may see your good works, and glorify your Father which is in heaven. Matthew 5:16

Pray that you will be able, not only to identify your gifts, but also to know how to implement them with maximum effectiveness. There are people to be reached with your gifts, people in both high and low places. And there are rewards to be received—if you will be willing to put your gifts to use.

What is your pursuit in life? Pursue your particular gift! It has rewards, both in this life and in the life to come. By using your gift for the benefit of those around you, you can become *A Man After God's Own Heart*. ♥

CHAPTER 9

UNDERSTANDING THE IMPORTANCE OF NOT SAVING YOUR OWN LIFE

A MAN AFTER GOD'S OWN HEART WOULD NEVER JEOPARDIZE THE
LIFE OF A FRIEND TO BENEFIT HIMSELF.

*And every one that was in distress, and every one that
was in debt, and every one that was discontented, gathered themselves unto him; and he became captain over
them: and there were with him about four hundred
men.*   1 Samuel 22:2

The story of David and his successes cannot be understood without understanding something of the men who
gathered themselves around him, making him their captain, and becoming fiercely loyal to him. There were
about four hundred of them, and they were not only with
him at the beginning. They were still with him at the
end.

Interestingly enough, they seemed to be little more
than a band of misfits. Saul certainly didn't want them.
To him, they were nothing more than outcasts, debtors,

and discontents. But after they had joined themselves to David in the wilderness, under his leadership they became something else entirely—men of strength. These were the men who made up David's private army, the men who accompanied him on his many daring forays for the Lord, the men who accompanied him when he rose to the throne.

These men would give anything for David—even their very lives if need be!

What David did they did. If he lived in the wilderness, they lived in the wilderness with him. When Absalom revolted against his father, and David was forced to flee, these men went with him. They were totally devoted to David. They would give anything for him—even their very lives if need be.

THE PROOF OF THEIR LOYALTY

As if to prove their loyalty, at one point, when David was in exile, he spoke aloud of thirsting for water from the well of Jerusalem. Whether he did this as a test of their loyalty or whether he was just thinking out loud is not clear. What is clear is that his men took his wish as a command and went off in search of the desired water.

Disregarding the danger to their own lives, they broke through the garrison of the Philistines, took water from the well, broke through the enemy garrison again on the return trip, and, finally, brought the water safely to David. What loyalty! What daring!

Joab was one of these men. He was so loyal to David that he sometimes disobeyed orders to do away with those he knew to be enemies of the king. He even killed Absalom, David's own son, after he had revolted against his father. He could not bear to see someone mistreat a man he knew to be as good as gold.

David's little band of men never once revolted against him. When they conquered any city, they called him to come and take charge of it. He could name that city whatever he liked and do with the spoils of it whatever he liked. The choice was his, for he was their captain.

THE DISLOYALTY OF ABSALOM

Absalom, on the other hand, David's own son, proved to be disloyal. He stole the hearts of his father's people, slept with his father's wives, and sought to take his father's throne and even his very life.

David had done nothing to deserve this treatment. When the shoe had been on the other foot, when he was waiting his turn to be king, he remained fiercely loyal to Saul—even when the man openly sought to do him harm. To David, Saul's life was very precious. To Absalom, his father deserved to die because he (Absalom) deserved to reign, and he had no more patience to wait his turn. The result was that he lost his chance to try.

We need never seek our own interest when we're serving others. Let their interests become our interests, and God will bless us for it. The moment we begin to seek our own interests and to put forward an independent and nonparticipating spirit, we have begun to be disloyal to our leadership, and God will never bless that attitude—no matter who exhibits it.

When David was exalted and became king over Israel, his men were exalted alongside him, and they became his *"mighty men."* Wait for your time and be loyal to others, and you, too, will be exalted.

After David's men brought the water to him, he couldn't bring himself to drink it. Instead, he poured it out as an offering unto the Lord. He could not bear the thought of jeopardizing the lives of others for the sake of his own. He was truly *A Man After God's Own Heart.*

WHO PAYS FOR YOUR SACRIFICE?

On another occasion, David refused to present an offering to God that cost him nothing:

> *All these things did Araunah, as a king, give unto the king [David]. And Araunah said unto the king, The lord thy God accept thee. And the king said unto Araunah, Nay; but I will surely buy it of thee at a price: neither will I offer burnt offerings unto the LORD my God of that which cost me nothing. So David bought the threshingfloor and the oxen for fifty shekels of silver.* 2 Samuel 24:23-24

David would not give an offering to God that did not cost him something, and he also would not allow someone else to pay for his sacrifice. What a man of God!

In the same way, Jesus was not willing to sell, or avoid in some way, the pain of the cross for some vinegar. It was His sacrifice to make, and He would make it.

Whatever you give to the Lord, let it come at your own sacrifice and not at the expense of others. The Lord hates robbery—especially when it comes to burnt offerings. Don't let your rise to authority be at the expense of others. Take them up with you and be blessed together. When you become selfless and stop working to make it all happen, then God will do it for you, for you will have become *A Man After God's Own Heart.* ♥

CHAPTER 10

LEARNING TO FOLLOW CHRIST'S EXAMPLE

A MAN AFTER GOD'S OWN HEART KNOWS THE IMPORTANCE OF FOLLOWING CHRIST'S EXAMPLE.

As my Father hath sent me, even so send I you.
                                                      John 20:21

In order to become a man after God's own heart, it is first necessary to do as Jesus commanded us, to be born again by His Spirit:

Therefore if any man be in Christ, he is a new creature: old things are passed away; behold, all things are become new.   2 Corinthians 5:17

If you are still a sinner, sold under the dominion of sin, the Scriptures show that your heart is *"deceitful"* and *"desperately"* wicked, so the first thing you need is a complete change of heart:

The heart is deceitful above all things, and desperately wicked: who can know it? Jeremiah 17:9

If you will just repent of your sins and accept Jesus into your heart as your Lord and Savior, your current life of sin will be changed into a life of righteousness. This is the redeeming work that Jesus came to earth to perform, and no one can change a life like He can. If you'll just give Him a chance, you'll be surprised at the change He can make in you.

BECOMING CHRIST-LIKE

Once we have accepted Jesus as our Lord and Savior, then our sights are set on becoming more and more like Him. David was a type of Christ, but only a type, a shadow, and not the real image. Jesus is the real thing. He is the perfect example of *A Man After God's Own* heart, and we must strive to be like Him. Paul wrote to the Ephesians:

But speaking the truth in love, may grow up into him in all things, which is the head even Christ.
Ephesians 4:15

God has blessed us with every spiritual blessing in heavenly places in Christ Jesus:

Blessed be the God and Father of our Lord Jesus Christ, who has blessed us with every spiritual blessing in the heavenly places in Christ. Ephesians 1:3

128

These spiritual blessings are given to us to make us blameless in the love of Christ. God long ago determined we should be adopted into His family and become His sons, possessing the same image as His only begotten Son.

Through the sacrifice of Jesus' blood, our God has redeemed us from every work of sin and Satan that should corrupt us and has forgiven us of all our sins. Therefore we can now become *"perfect,"* even as our Father in Heaven is perfect:

> *Be ye therefore perfect, even as your Father which is in heaven is perfect.*
>
> Matthew 5:48

We can love as Jesus loved, and we can obey our heavenly Father as He obeyed His heavenly Father. We can make His will our will and His work our work. Jesus expressed this potential when He declared: *"As my Father hath sent me, even so send I you."* The Father sent Him, and now He is sending you and me.

Once we have accepted Jesus as our Lord and Savior, then our sights are set on becoming more and more like Him!

CHRIST HAD AN ESTABLISHED MINISTRY

Regarding a continued and establish ministry, there is no better example than that of Jesus Himself. He prepared Himself for thirty years and then conducted His ministry for just three and a half years. In the more than two thousand years that have transpired since then, Christianity has established itself as the largest and fastest growing faith in the world. If we can learn from Jesus' example and obey His voice, our own ministries (which are really a continuation of His ministry) will also prosper and outlive us.

In Christ, we can live a life and ministry free from condemnation:

There is therefore now no condemnation to them who are IN CHRIST JESUS.   Romans 8:1

For we are His workmanship, created IN CHRIST JESUS unto good works.   Ephesians 2:20

But of him are ye IN CHRIST JESUS, who of God is made unto us wisdom, and righteousness, and sanctification and redemption.   1 Corinthians 1:30

If we choose to obey Him and live by His Word, we can be free from every form of condemnation. Therefore abide in Him, for *"in him we live, and move, and have our being"* (Acts 17:28). *"We are his offspring"* (same verse). We are made in His image and likeness, we have His mind, we are His Body, and have been given His Spirit. So let us go forth into this world and continue our ministry until we are established and made captain in God's house, laying a foundation and making a mark upon our generation. In this way, we will prove ourselves as *A Man After God's Own Heart.* ♥

Scripture Passages Used

Chapter 2: *Why Did God Choose David to Replace Saul?*

1. 1 Samuel 16:6-7
2. Psalm 44:2
3. Psalm 42:1-2
4. 1 Samuel 16:12-13
5. Matthew 6:18
6. Matthew 6:33
7. 1 Samuel 16:17-18
8. Psalm 111:10
9. 2 Corinthians 5:17
10. Romans 12:1-2
11. Jeremiah 17:9
12. Ecclesiastes 11:9
13. Matthew 15:17-20
14. Matthew 6:21
15. 1 John 3:9
16. Matthew 12:34-35
17. John 4:23-24
18. Proverbs 4:23
19. 2 Peter 1:10
20. 2 Peter 1:5-6

Chapter 3: *Understanding Your Covenant with God*

1. 1 Samuel 17:26
2. Proverbs 18:16
3. Hebrews 12:2
4. 1 Samuel 17:26-27

5. Ecclesiastes 9:11
6. Ecclesiastes 3:11
7. Proverbs 23:7
8. 1 Samuel 17:26
9. Psalm 1:3
10. Deuteronomy 32:30
11. Psalm 34:7
12. 1 Samuel 17:28-29
13. Deuteronomy 33:25
14. Psalm 118:17
15. Colossians 2:13-15
16. 2 Peter 1:3-4
17. Proverbs 24:16
18. Romans 8:38-39

Chapter 4: *Learning To Inquire of God*

1. 1 Samuel 23:6, 9-12
2. Psalm 37:23
3. Proverbs 19:21
4. 1 Samuel 30:8
5. Luke 15:6
6. 2 Samuel 5:19
7. 2 Samuel 5:23-24
8. John 16:13

Chapter 5: *Relating Your Covenant with God to Man*

1. 1 Samuel 18:1 & 3
2. Matthew 5:48

3. Luke 6:31
4. 1 Samuel 18:4
5. 2 Samuel 9:3-4
6. 1 Samuel 9:6-8
7. Daniel 2:21
8. John 8:7
9. Matthew 18:33
10. 2 Samuel 21:7
11. John 13:35

Chapter 6: *Learning Not to Avenge Yourself of Your Enemies*

1. 1 Samuel 26:9
2. 1 Samuel 24:4-7
3. Psalm 105:15
4. Deuteronomy 32:35
5. 1 Samuel 24:12
6. Matthew 26:52-53
7. Luke 23:34
8. 1 Samuel 26:9
9. Romans 14:4
10. 2 Chronicles 3:1
11. 2 Samuel 4:10-11
12. Isaiah 54:17
13. Luke 10:19
14. Matthew 5:43-45
15. 2 Samuel 1:19-20
16. Romans 5:8

Chapter 7: *Being Willing to Confessing and Forsaking Your Sins*

1. Psalm 51:1-3
2. 1 John 2:1-2
3. 2 Corinthians 12:10
4. Proverbs 28:13

Chapter 8: *Determining to Build God's House*

1. 1 Samuel 7:1-3
2. Acts 2:29-31
3. Psalm 40:6-7
4. 2 Samuel 24:25
5. Psalm 2:2-3
6. Acts 2:31
7. Psalm 67:4
8. 2 Chronicles 8:14
9. Acts 17:24-26
10. 2 Samuel 7:8-16
11. Luke 6:38
12. Galatians 6:7
13. 2 Samuel 6:14-16, 20 & 23
14. 2 Samuel 6:21-22
15. Matthew 5:16

Chapter 9: *Understanding the Importance of Not Saving Your Own Life*

1. 1 Samuel 22:2
2. 2 Samuel 24:23-24

Chapter 10: *Learning from Christ's Example*

1. John 20:21
2. 2 Corinthians 5:17
3. Jeremiah 17:7
4. Ephesians 4:15
5. Ephesians 1:3
6. Matthew 5:48
7. Romans 8:1
8. Ephesians 2:20
9. 1 Corinthians 1:30
10. Acts 17:28   ♥

ALPHABETIZED INDEX OF SCRIPTURES USED

MINISTRY PAGE

Those wishing to correspond with the author may do so at the following addresses:

In Africa:
Pastor Desmond A. Thomas
Ministry of the Word
P.M.B. 365
Freetown, Sierra Leone
West Africa

In Europe:
Ministry of the Word
desmondthomasministries@yahoo.com
www.desmondthomas.org

In the U.S.:
Ministry of the Word
c/o McDougal & Associates
www.thepublishedword.com

Printed in the United Kingdom
by Lightning Source UK Ltd.
129665UK00001B/58-90/P